I0098831

SPOUSE OVER THE HOUSE
OR
MOUSE IN THE HOUSE

Family Series Book # 1

For Fathers, Married Couples, Parents, Grandparents, Singles of All Ages, Children, Newlyweds and Budgeting

By Dr. Fred Jerkins Jr.

DEDICATION

=================================

I dedicate this book to my wife "Sylvia" who I have been married to for fifty five years. Sylvia gives me the space and time to write books. When I get a little slack, she motivates me to re-start. I also dedicate this book to my four children; Sharene, Sybil and Fred III and Rodney and their wives Shannon and Joy.

I also dedicate this book to all our grandchildren, great grandchildren, siblings, nieces, nephews, cousins, and our living aunts and uncles.

I finally dedicate this book to all our spiritual sons and daughters and to our friends, those that are in the ministry and those that are not in the ministry.

I dedicate this book.

CONTENTS

==

INTRODUCTION

This book will address some of our 21st century problems and several solutions to those problems. The material contained is drawn from the accumulated knowledge gained from 59 years of being in the, ministry, 55 years of marriage and 50 years as a pastor. As a pastor, I have counselled with families and married couples for years. In addition, I have studied the word of God for many years and have utilized principles from God's word in my counseling sessions. One can draw many valuable principles from the ancient Jewish culture and from Biblical perspectives.

This perspective is definitely needed today when marriages and families are in deep trouble. Non-Christian as well as Christian marriages in our modern-day society are suffering. The statistic on the separation and divorce rate is about fifty-fifty percent. Which means that fifty percent of everyone who gets married ultimately ends up divorced or separated. If something does not alter these trends, the marriage institution as we know it may end up extinct.

There are benefits to reading this book, it not only addresses several problems of our day, but it gives you tools and principles to use to reverse damaged relationships. In addition, it gives you the needed practical methods and Biblical principles to assist you in restoring and resurrecting your marriage and family relationships.

This book is different than many other books out there today because it does not just deal with the Male Spouse Being Over The House, It deals with the elevation of the Female Spouse, it deals with marriage situations, it addresses the difficulties that are affecting and infecting the whole family in our day and it provides practical biblical solutions.

The entire 21ˢᵗ century family structure is in trouble. Many young children are being neglected in so many ways. Our teenagers, young adults and millennials are in need of solid direction and guidance from the Holy Scriptures, as do our baby boomers and some of our senior citizens.

What I am attempting to do in this book, is to give to you all a true Godly and moral foundation from God's Word. Moreover, the Word of God applied in your life will serve as a mechanism to combat the teachings of humanism and secularism, which are being taught in our schools, colleges and universities.

This book gives a holistic approach not only for dealing with our children, teenagers and young adults, but for singles of all age groups, married couples of all age groups, parents, grandparents, and great grandparents.

Our homes are in dire trouble because many of the fathers, within all cultures, are not there. Many children are either trying to raise themselves, or a mom is raising them alone because the father is absent. Alternatively, there are other children being raised by their grandparents, the great grandparents, a relative or a guardian.

I am praying that this book, along with the Holy Bible, help and assist you parents in raising your children and in solidifying your marriage and family relationships. I am praying that this book along with God's Holy Word, will guide and help you singles in your marriage decisions in life.

When you read, practice and follow fully, on a daily basis, the Biblical principles written in this book, your family relationships will become stronger.

This book can also serve as a manual to guide pastors and counselors as they deal with a myriad of problems in the family during this 21st century.

As you read my first book in this family series *Spouse Over the House or Mouse in the House,* be blessed of God as your family relationships grow. God Bless!

~ PART ONE ~

SYMBOLISM
PEOPLE LIKE ANIMALS

Upon studying the Holy Scriptures, I noticed that God and other Biblical writers many times spoke about a particular animal in order to describe the different aspects of the character of a human being. Some characteristics and behavior of certain animals seem to mirror the very characteristic of a person or some people. Therefore, when a person is referred to as an animal in the Bible, it is not literal. That person is referred to as an animal either metaphorically or symbolically. On the other hand, he may be referred to *figuratively* as a particular animal.

A metaphor is a comparison made between two or more things using figurative or descriptive language. Metaphors serve to make difficult to understand ideas or concepts more tangible. Metaphors were a literary device commonly used in the Bible.

The Bible is full of symbols, but just in case you do not know what symbols are, below is a definition of what Bible symbols are:

Symbols are a path to revelation. A Biblical symbol is a word in the Bible that has a deeper alternative meaning that is in addition to the plain, and obvious meaning. The alternative meaning is the "Symbolic Meaning" or "Symbolic Definition". God designed it to give some texts a deeper, alternative meaning. Biblical symbol definitions are defined by other Bible texts. The Bible defines every Bible symbol, or it is not a true Bible symbol.

> *Biblical Symbols are keys to shine new light on old doctrine. Symbolism is the vehicle of revelation.*

Now let's look at several examples in the Holy Scripture where God/Jesus or a writer refers to an animal in order to describe the character of a person.

A Fox: Jesus referred to Herod the Great as a fox. A fox is sly, cunning and destructive; a suspicious, unclean animal. However, in the Hebrew culture, a fox was described with more than just those five characteristics.

The Context: Jesus' characterization of Herod as a fox is a story that appears in *Luke 13:31-33*:

At that time, some Pharisees came to Jesus and said to him, "Leave this place and go somewhere else. Herod wants to kill you." He replied, "Go tell that fox, 'I will drive out demons and heal people today and tomorrow, and on the third day I will reach my goal.' In any case, I must keep going today and tomorrow and the next day for surely no prophet can die outside Jerusalem!"

A commentary on these verses: Jesus drew closer and closer to the holy city — the city that would ultimately witness his execution on the cross — and he continued to teach, heal, and proclaim God's sovereignty over a world increasingly hostile to God's love. Aware of the growing tension and nervous anticipation surrounding the sacred festival in Jerusalem, some Pharisees sought him out with what appears to be a dire warning. "Get out of Jerusalem," they urgently warned him. "Herod wants to kill you!"

Undaunted, Jesus responded with seemingly uncharacteristic insults and prophetic proclamations. Jesus boldly responds to the Pharisees referring to King Herod as a fox and then goes on to essentially say that he will not be intimidated by the idle threats of a rich aristocrat who is more concerned with power and wealth than fulfilling God's ministry.

In the Jewish culture of Jesus' time, to call someone a fox was to say that person was a liar, an imposter, or someone who was too slimy and conniving to be trusted. It was an in-your-face slam against the established ruler of Galilee, King Herod.

11

Jesus was calling the king a liar, a cheat and a worthless imposter who deceives and corrupts the people with his arrogance.

There are many places in the Bible where a person is symbolically or metaphorically characterized as an animal in order for you to see their true nature. There are times when nations and people are figuratively named as an animal or beast. Here are few:

Dog: The Bible describes some people like undomesticated wild dogs. *Psalm 22:16, Proverbs 26:11, Philippians 3:2, Revelation 22:15 and Isaiah 56:10-11.*

Swine and Dogs: *Matthew 7:6 KJV; 2 Peter 2:22*

Wolf and Wolves: Beware of false prophets. *Matthew 7:15, John 10:12*

Sheep and Goats: My sheep - *John10:27*. The judgment of the living nations, he shall separate the sheep from the goats. *Matthew 25:31-46*

Lamb: Jesus is the Lamb of God, *John 1:29*, which taketh away the sins of the world.

Dove: The Dove - The Holy Spirit was described figuratively as being like a dove - *Luke 3:22*

Eagle and Eagle's wings: An eagle is a symbol of sight, strength, endurance Exodus *19:4-6. Duet 32:11, Psalm 103:5, Isaiah 40:31.*

The Bear, Leopard, Lion and Ten Horned Beast: Daniel 7:2-8 and *Revelation 13:2* Beast: *Ecclesiastes 3:18-19* Ten Horn Beasts: *Revelation 17:12.*

The Serpent: the Dragon is Satan...*Rev 12:9; 20:2, Revelation 12:9.*

As you can see, there are many symbols of animas in the Holy Scriptures. These animals characterize how different people mimic animals in their behavior.

Nevertheless, in this book we want to only present how a man, particularly a husbandman acts like a mouse sometimes. Some of the characteristics that he exhibits are some of the same characteristics exhibited by the mouse.

A. LET'S OBSERVE THE NEGATIVE TRAITS OF THE MOUSE:

1. A mouse is a rodent; it is a pest, which can get on one's nerves because of its behavior.

2. When you observed the anatomy and the skeletal system of a mouse- It doesn't have the needed *backbone* – known as the shoulders. However, this works for the mouse because, it enables it to squeeze itself into places where he is not wanted, it allows it to *squeeze* through a crack that's the size of a nickel. Nevertheless, with no *backbone*, when it becomes fearful, it will swiftly run to its crack to escape any known threat.

3. A mouse is skittish - it is their timidity and fear that forces them to keep a low profile. A mouse is uncomfortable when it is exposed openly.

4. A mouse is a non-competitive animal, it does not like the challenge to do things differently in order to get ahead.

A mouse with its small personality, finds it difficult to compete in the business world.

5. A mouse is a *HOARDER*; mice are manic about hoarding their resources while planning.

If anyone were to look inside a mouse's "garage" they would be struck by the mountains of old newspapers, boxes and broken tools piled to the ceiling. These objects represent security and peace of mind for the mouse, and parting with them would be like separating from a lover. Consequently, they are often seen scurrying around swap meets and garage sales, eagerly adding to their collection.

A mouse is a thief; it is a cheese eating thief! It will risk being caught in a 'mouse trap' rather than doing it the right way. Some men are like mice, they'd rather steal their provision instead of following God's blessing plan for their provision.

Lastly, a mouse is a dangerous destructive pest, because they carry and transmit viruses, bacteria and other diseases. Some men are like mice, they contaminate those whom they are with constantly.

~ PART TWO ~
FAMILY PROBLEMS

Every marriage today is suffering or dealing with some type of problem, and as result of those problems the entire family living in the home - the small children, the teenager and the young adult - are affected in a negative way.

Every family and every marriage will have trouble and setbacks and if they are not dealt with in a proper wholesome manner, that family relationship ultimately disintegrates.

Some couples and some families spend too much time arguing and disputing over stupid stuff, only to realize later that it would have been better to just be quiet, ignore it and leave it alone. The problem, so insignificant, did not deserve that much negative attention in the first place.

Then there are other times when the problem(s) is real, serious and very painful and it deserves some positive attention and solutions in order to bring correction and healing. No marriage is perfect. No one has a perfect human family.

The Father First: The Bible teaches that the father is first, as the God ordained leading parent, to love his children, provide for his children, train up his children, educate and protect his children from immorality, heathen, pagan religions and wrong marriages.

The responsibility to protect a son and a daughter from heathenism and paganism was first given to the Jewish father in the Old Testament. As a result, it was their custom and culture to have arranged marriages for their sons and daughters. By the approval of the father of the bride to be and the acceptance of the proposal by the daughter, then and only then the betrothal period (the engagement period) would begin.

Example:
When the Lord thy God shall bring thee into the land whither thou goest to possess it, and hath cast out many nations before thee, the Hittites, and the Girgashites, and the Amorites, and the Canaanites, and the Perizzites, and the Hivites, and the Jebusites, seven nations greater and mightier than thou;

And when the Lord thy God shall deliver them before thee; thou shalt smite them, and utterly destroy them; thou shalt make no covenant with them, nor shew mercy unto them:

Neither shalt thou make marriages with them; thy daughter thou shalt not give unto his son, nor his daughter shalt thou take unto thy son. (Deuteronomy 7:1-3)

The story of the marriage of Isaac and Rebekah (*Gen. 24*) is a rich Biblical source for studying marriage practices and customs in the ancient world. The story begins with Abraham's instructions to his servant to bring a wife for his son. The servant chose Rebekah from among Abraham's people, the people of God. *(Deuteronomy 7:3)*

The Problem - Absentee Dads – *Kids Need a Role Model*: A mother is not a father; a mother cannot be a father or take the place of a father. This is not a put down of those wonderful God-fearing moms who are rearing their children in a fatherless home. There are certain Biblical requirements and responsibilities that God has placed upon each father. Moreover, if that father shirks/neglects those responsibilities, he becomes just a *Mouse in the House and not the Spouse Over His House*.

Kids Need a Role Model: I reiterate what I said previously, those obligations to do certain things lie upon the father *first*. As the leader of his household, he is the *first role model* to his female spouse and to his sons and daughters.

He is the *first* one that God gave the responsibility to provide for his children, train his children and educate his children. He is to protect his children by passing on - transferring fatherly family blessings.

Problem - No Father Role Model: When the dad is physically absent there is no male *role model* in the home. Some fathers who are present in the home setting still do not know how to be a real father because he never had his father in his life. Many sons were raised without a dad as a role model.

Many fathers are not there for their children for many reasons; some are not there because of separation or divorce. Some are not there because they are incarcerated. Others are not there because they are hooked on drugs. Some are not there because they are just deadbeat dads and do not want to be there for a wife and children because it is too much of a responsibility. Some fathers are not there for their sons and daughters because they only want to be a baby daddy with children born out of wedlock. On the other hand, some fathers are not there for their family because they have been driven away by an *overbearing, overruling*, female spouse.

On the other side of this scenario, a father can be there but not there. What do I mean? Allow me to explain. There are fathers across this country, in the world and in the church who are living in the home but not there because they have disconnected themselves mentally, emotionally, volitionally and spiritually from their children.

Although they live in the home with their children, they have abandoned their fatherly duties completely. As a result, in some cases, a child rebels until he or she gravitates towards evil devices and things that God describes as an abomination. It is the father's fault. He is to blame for not being there for his children. Whatever the reason for this epidemic of fatherless homes in this 21st century, it is a sad commentary.

Children need their father in their lives. There is also much emotional pain suffered by those sons and daughters who experience the vacancy of their father.

I remember a few years ago, when I was conducting a men's seminar, near the end of the talk, I noticed an older man crying like a baby. He came up front with tears streaming down his face. He said: "Pastor, can I talk with you?" I answered, yes! He said: "I never had my father in my life, I needed my father. I wanted my father, but he was never there for our family and me". I literally felt his pain. As a younger man "I grabbed him, hugged him and said as of today, "*I will be your father*". As a father figure, I expressed to him that I loved him and that I was proud of him. I continued to tell him that he always had a true father in Heaven.

God said in his Word, that he would be a father to the fatherless in a special, supernatural way that no earthly father could ever fulfill. That older man dried his eyes and began to smile as though that day was life changing for him.

God is: A father of the fatherless, and a judge of the widows, is God in his holy habitation (Psalm 68:5-6)

Here is another story; there was a young man who lived in a Christian home with two Christian parents. Nevertheless, it was evident that the father was dealing with some known and unknown issues in his life. Moreover, for some odd reason he would always put down this son. He would tell him that he was no good and that he would never amount to anything. The father never had any good or positive thing to say to his son.

That young man, when he was around nineteen years old, left home feeling unloved by his father and gravitated towards the wrong crowd. He got involved in worldly sins and vices.

Consequently, he took sick and ended up in the hospital; his sickness was unto death. One day I visited him and lead him to the Lord. As I talked with him, he shared with me before he passed away that all he ever wanted was his father to tell him that he *loved* him!

Another well-known, mega minister only had one child who was a daughter. He was so busy in the ministry with other folk and their children until he neglected his own daughter. He never spent any precious, private times with his daughter when she was young or even as she became a teenager. It left a vacuum inside of her, an unexplainable emptiness. His neglect of her when she needed him most left a deep wound in her heart. The scripture states that a wounded heart is hard to be healed. He took sick, and on his deathbed, he tried to patch things up. However, it was too late to rebuild the long-neglected relationship.

These three, true stories bring tears to my eyes every time I think about them or share them with others. Lord, please guide me and other dads and grand dads out there, to be there with love and support for our sons, daughters, grandchildren and great grandchildren.

These three stories are being repeated time and time again in many family lives today. Children need and want their fathers. Oh, how I wish and pray that these absentee dads could only realize how bad they are needed in their sons' and daughters' lives. I beg you, please do not be just *a mouse in your house*, but the *God ordained spouse over your house.*

The Male is The Authority Figure in The House: As a role model, the male spouse was also given by God the position of leadership, headship, and the authority figure in the home. Whether his female spouse likes his position or disagrees with his God given position, it does not matter. The scriptures say that the man is the head of the woman and the man is the head of his wife.

But I would have you know, that the head of every man is Christ; and the head of the woman is the man; and the head of Christ is God. (1 Corinthians 11:3-10)

For the husband is the head of the wife, even as Christ is the head of the church: and he is the savior of the body. (Ephesian 5:23) (Notice the husband is the *head of his wife*! - The word spouse is a synonym that represents the husband or a wife.)

Definition of a Spouse

A spouse is your companion, your mate and your partner. In the olden times, spouse was used as a verb, meaning "to marry," but nowadays, it functions as a noun referring to either husband or wife. Therefore, when you are married, there are two spouses in the house, the male spouse and the female spouse.

Notice: The designated position of the male spouse from this Scripture, Ephesian 5:23, is: he is the *Head Spouse in the House* and *over the household*. In addition, he is supposed to be respected and obeyed as thus in those things that are right.

Wives, submit yourselves unto your own husbands, as unto the Lord. (Ephesians 5:22-33)

Wives, submit yourselves unto your own husbands, as it is fit in the Lord. (Col. 3:18)

Moreover, because of his God given position of headship, he is the first leader under God, the first home ruler that God has ordained to rule his entire household, which includes his biological children or his adopted children. In addition, he is to rule over his wife in love with the guidance and direction of God Almighty through the Holy Scriptures. The dad is to be a *role model,* an example, not by talk alone, but by walking in the ways of God.

He is never supposed to act like a mouse by becoming so fearful and timid of his surrounding until he takes off and runs away from his responsibilities.

One Trait of a Mouse is Timidity

As the male spouse over your house, God chose you to be the provider for your family. Moreover, in order to provide, you must work. Too many men today are just "dead beat dads" who do not want to work, but rather stay home, watch TV, play games, spend most of their time on social media sites while life and golden opportunities are passing them by.

Sometimes, his excuse for not working is because he claims to be either under qualified for the position he desires or over qualified. But that is not an excuse for not working on a job somewhere. *(2 Thessalonians 3:10-12)*

For even when we were with you, this we commanded you, that if any would not work, neither should he eat.

For we hear that there are some which walk among you disorderly, working not at all, but are busybodies.

Now them that are such we command and exhort by our Lord Jesus Christ, that with quietness they work, and eat their own bread.

Mouse Traits: Another trait of a mouse he is non-competitive. He never does anything different to compete in order to win in life and therefore he never excels from where he is.

Like the mouse, the weak spouse, his only motivation, his only passion is to keep doing the same thing repeatedly even if it's not getting anything but the same negative results. As long as he operates in *his own house like a mouse*, he will never gain the competitive edge in employment and in business.

Like a Mouse: He is a hoarder of scraps, but does not invest his time, his money and his energy into real ventures, properties and businesses that will bring him blessed dividends. I have met men like that; once they get paid, they spend all their money on scraps and gadgets and never save real money for a rainy day, an emergency or for investments. They get paid on Friday, and by Monday, they are broke. They do not have bus fare, car fare or transportation to get to their job.

A good spouse knows that he must work in order to eat, in order to provide for his wife and children. One of the goals that he sets in life is to acquire employment even if he must become an entrepreneur or a self-contractor.

As the spouse over the house and the first role model of the household, the husband is not only supposed to seek to meet the needs of his children, but also the needs of his wife; providing shelter, food and clothing for his family members. As a husband and spouse, he has a duty to be sensitive to the physical, mental, emotional and spiritual needs of his wife.

To meet her physical need, he is to be the provider of the home. He is to seek to provide a house for their shelter (a nice house where they can be comfortable). He is to provide the money for clothing and food. He is to seek to provide money for their rest and vacation time.

Your wife also has emotional needs. There are some basic and mega needs of a female spouse, here are a few: security, love, respect, appreciation and attention.

Attention is a basic and mega need of a female, a woman, a wife. She wants you to notice her, what she is wearing, how she looks, here perfume, what she does for you and the family.

She needs your attention on her, and she needs your attention often! She needs you to be verbal about how you love her, respect her and appreciate her. She needs you to compliment her often.

Moreover, when any one of these needs are neglected on any level, especially "*attention*", it will create some friction in the marital relationship. Therefore, I will repeat, she needs to know that you love her romantically above all others. True love breeds respect; she needs you to respect her at all times, in private and in the public. She also needs to know and feel that her marriage is secure, regardless of the problems and challenges you both might incur.

Again, she needs appreciation and attention. When she prepares a great meal for you and the family, or run errands for you and the family, do not take it for granted. As you give her your undivided attention at various times, thank her often for what she does for you and the family. It is so easy to be critical and find fault in things that she is not doing, but I suggest that you focus on the wonderful things that she *is* doing.

Incidentally, when you, the male spouse, run away or simply avoid meeting her needs, you are not acting like the *Spouse who is Over the House* but just a *Mouse in the House.*

Men Have Needs Too: To you wives out there, the number one need of your husband is *honor and respect.* He needs his wife to honor and respect him in the public arena and at home in the house. He needs you to show honor and respect in your speech, your attitude, your actions and your facial expressions. In addition, he has a dominant sexual appetite that he needs you to fulfill. When you fail in this area with such a mega need, you have blown it big time.

Female Spouse - Mouth Problem: The male spouse many times cannot fulfill his God given purpose in his own house because he is being dishonored and disrespected in his home. Sometimes the female spouse can have a "toxic tongue" and she assassinates her husband with her mouth. It is verbal abuse. She verbalizes her refusal to allow him to be the first leader of the household.

Consequently, *her mouth drives him into behaving like a mouse in the house instead of the spouse over his house.* Many wives of our day have a secret desire to rule over their husbands. Dishonor and disrespect will drive a good spouse away.

In this 21st century society within some circles, women are gaining dominant control over men. It seems as though America is heading toward becoming a matriarchal or feminist society. This un-natural need for some females to dominate men is not only in the world, but it is in the political arena among many women. We have observed this desire to dominate men among liberation feminist groups. These attitudes to dominate and to rule men have influenced many religious and Christian denominations.

Within some denominations, this attitude of female domination can be seen in the home as well as in ministry. Moreover, it has created a major problem in the home for the husband and children. Consequently, it has created major problems in ministry.

The feminist rejects the idea of men being the head. They are in a power struggle. They are demanding equality on every level. However, their real, obvious goal is to dominate, control and rule over men. They have a desire to rule all men including their husband. God said in Genesis the third chapter, that this desire to rule men would happen.

Genesis 3:16 which records the curse of Eve is in two parts;
1) She will suffer *physical pain* in childbirth. 2) *She will have a desire to rule:*

Eve lost that equality of being co-ruler over everything along with her husband Adam after they sinned. It is in our nature, our soul and in our DNA to sin.

We inherited the sin nature. In addition, I believe that it is in the woman's DNA or in her soul to fulfill also that part of her curse to periodically desire to rule over her husband and/or over men.

The loss of her being a co-ruler resulted in her having conflicting desires:

1. A desire to rule sometimes, and a desire to be ruled.
2. A desire to dominate men, particularly her husband sometimes, and a desire to be *dominated* by her husband at other times.
3. A desire to exert control and rule over her husband at times and at other times she desires for him to exert control over her.

In this area of her life, she experiences ups and downs - swings of emotions. These melancholy emotions confuse most men. Because of this mental, emotional and volitional part of her curse for eating of the tree first and then leading her husband into sin, the female spouse can act melancholy at different times concerning her position. In fact, she often uses the term that our relationship is 50-50 (equal control in everything). Again, *1 Corinthians 11:3* and *Ephesian 5:23* as well as other scriptures teach that men are the head of the woman, and the husband is the head of his wife.

You must understand that these scriptures reveal a part of God's divine order of the chain of authority. Moreover, God is not a chauvinist nor is he a misogynistic God.

These scriptures above will irritate a *rebellious* wife. My commentary on this; because of this part of the curse, (the desire to rule) is the *real reason* why we see women struggling, arguing and fighting for control.

For those women and wives who do not have the correct interpretations and understanding of *Genesis 3:16*, they feel that they are operating in their God ordained position as a co-ruler or ruler over men. They believe that God is doing a 'new thing' in the earth realm in these last days, and one of those new things is their right to rule.

As I previously stated, the attitudes of domination and ruling over the husband has spilled over into Christianity. Moreover, some Christian women are destroying their homes because they refuse to subject themselves under the obedience of their husband.

Again, one of a husband's mega need is honor and respect. You blow it completely when you do not meet that need. When a female spouse's attitude is disrespectful and bossy, she is dishonoring her male spouse.

These attitudes of her desire to rule are portrayed in a bossy and disobedient disposition. The new widespread rebellion we are observing in our society today has not been witnessed in past marital history on this scale. Many women and wives of all cultures and ethnic backgrounds, regardless of their educational status, are becoming as stubborn as a mule and refuse to allow the man, the husband, to fulfill his God-ordained position.

Once the female spouse inwardly decides that she is not going to allow her male spouse to rule over her or his house any longer, this is when real trouble begins. She begins to use her tongue as a weapon against him.

Her tongue and her mouth become like a dagger, a sword, or even a razor in her home against her husband. The slander, the put downs, the verbal lashing and condescending remarks drives him into a menial, mouse-like position.

Once this *ruling attitude* dominates her, she will then begin verbally assassinating her husband in private and in public in front of friends and foes. Consequently, it weakens his position. She seems to be in opposition to everything he does. Instead of him receiving approvals from her, it is a constant disapproval. Instead of her building him up or strengthening him, she tears him down. She is constantly fussing at him not realizing that she is literally driving him away.

Her constant dominance of him ultimately drives him into a menial, weak and non- ruling position. Because he does not want to fight back against the verbal attacks and verbal insults, he gives in. Because he does not want others to know that he is losing his control, he gives up! He tried using soft answers as a defense mechanism but with her it seems like it is not working.

Psalm 52:2-3: The tongue deviseth mischiefs; like a sharp razor, working deceitfully.

Observe what James the Apostle said concerning putting a bridle on the tongue: James 3:5-12 (KJV)
5 Even so the tongue is a little member, and boasteth great things. Behold, how great a matter a little fire kindleth!

6 And the tongue is a fire, a world of iniquity: so is the tongue among our members, that it defileth the whole body, and setteth on fire the course of nature; and it is set on fire of hell.

7 For every kind of beasts, and of birds, and of serpents, and of things in the sea, is tamed, and hath been tamed of mankind:

8 But the tongue can no man tame; it is an unruly evil, full of deadly poison.

⁹ *Therewith bless we God, even the Father; and therewith curse we men, which are made after the similitude of God.*

¹⁰ *Out of the same mouth proceedeth blessing and cursing. My brethren, these things ought not so to be.*

¹¹ *Doth a fountain send forth at the same place sweet water and bitter?*

¹² *Can the fig tree, my brethren, bear olive berries? either a vine, figs? so can no fountain both yield salt water and fresh.*

Notice also Proverbs 21:23 *"Whoso keepeth his mouth and his tongue keepeth his soul from troubles."*

Coupled with using her mouth to boss her spouse around, some wives go a step further by refusing to allow her husband to make love to her sexually unless she gets what she wants, or he meets her demands. Now she is holding him hostage.

King Ahab allowed Jezebel to gain control over him. Consequently, she led him in rebellion against the commandments of God (*1Kings 21:25*). Also, the Persian King Ahasuerus' wife, Queen Vashti, tried to gain control over him but she failed and was banned from the kingdom, resulting in Esther becoming the King's wife and the new Queen of the kingdom. (*Esther 1: 12-19*)

The loud mouth, rebellious wife sometimes gain full control over her spouse. Her attitude and her mouth drive her husband into being just a M*ouse in the House* instead of the *Spouse Over the House.*

To add insult to Injury, while he is now operating from a defeated position, she tells him sometimes, "Why don't you stand up and be a man"; "If you are a man, then act like a man!"

Again, God said in Genesis 3:16:

Unto the woman he said, I will greatly multiply thy sorrow and thy conception; in sorrow, thou shalt bring forth children; and thy desire shall be to thy husband, and he shall rule over thee.

Her desire shall be to her husband - is not speaking of sexual desire, it is the desire to *rule over him.* How we know this is because of what God tells her next in terms of what will eventually happen, he said: but he shall rule over thee. A strong man will bounce back; a weak man will give up his control.

Women Ruling Over Men Humbled By God:
Seven Women Chasing One Man (Isaiah 4:1)

In Prophet Isaiah's day, the men and women of Zion had backslidden against God, walked away from holiness, living in pride and rebellion, building and worshipping idol gods that they made with their own hands.

According to Isaiah 3:12 the women of Zion were living in such rebellion until they were literally ruling over the men. In addition, they were allowing their children, the younger generation to oppress the older people. They erred by allowing their children, their sons and daughters, their young people to disrespect and dishonor the elderly by extortion for unjust gain.

As for my people, children are their oppressors, and women rule over them. O my people, they which lead thee cause thee to err, and destroy the way of thy paths. (Isaiah 3:12)

The prophet Isaiah records, how the women in their pride, walked around with a haughty spirit. They dressed and acted like they were above the rest of the people.

Moreover, the Lord saith, Because the daughters of Zion are haughty, and walk with stretched forth necks and wanton eyes, walking and mincing as they go, and making a tinkling with their feet. (Isaiah 3:16-18)

[17]Therefore the Lord will smite with a scab the crown of the head of the daughters of Zion, and the Lord will discover their secret parts.

[18] In that day the Lord will take away the bravery of their tinkling ornaments about their feet, and their cauls and their round tires like the moon.

God sent Isaiah the Prophet to prophesy against the backslidden men of Israel and Judah. In addition, he told him to prophesy against those haughty prideful women, those who were now ruling over men.

God made it prophetically clear that he was sending his judgment against those backslidden men, backslidden women and backslidden young people who were abusing the elderly. The only alternative God gave to them was to repent and turn from their wicked, rebellious ways or suffer the consequence of his judgment. This judgment would bring the male population down because the sword would destroy most of them and the mighty men will be killed in the coming war of judgment.

After this destruction, the male population will be so depleted, until the women of Zion shall be left living in desperation, desiring and seeking after a man to marry, in order to give her his name, in order take away her reproach. In those days, it was a reproach for a woman not to have a husband.

The judgment of God was going to be so severe that it will cause these "haughty ruling women" to lose all their pride.
The scripture says in that day, the day after most men of Judah are killed, the women will become so *desperate* until seven women will chase *one* man.

Notice what this scripture says:

*And in that day **seven women** shall take hold of one man, saying, we will eat our own bread, and wear our own apparel: only let us be called by thy name, to take away our reproach. (Isaiah 4:1 KJV)*

The word of God is clear; it states that God is going to judge those women of Judah. In addition, his judgment will ultimately humble them. They will be humbled to the point until seven women will beg one man to marry them.

My commentary is this; God was saying when I get through bringing judgment, there shall be a "man shortage" in Zion - so much so until consequently, these rebellious, prideful women will get to the point of desperation. They will be willing to submit their lives to a life of polygamy without becoming jealous of the other women who will be married to the same man.

That day was fulfilled in Judah's history. 2 Chronicles 28:6 records that *one hundred and twenty thousand* men were killed in one day. *2 Chronicles 28:8* also records that two hundred thousand women, sons and daughter were taken captive. Their spoils (their belongings) were carried away into Samaria also.

Prophecy Fulfilled: The prophecy was fulfilled; the war brought about a man shortage and seven women, which again signifies a very large number of women, became so desperate until they lost their pride and seven of them (or a large number of them) began to chase after one man begging him to marry them in order to take away their reproach.

Desperate Women: We have a new problem in our day, some women of our world, including some church going women, are living in desperation. They sincerely desire to be married. Nevertheless, it is not because the female population is out-numbering the men, seven to one.

However, it is because our twenty first century society is so divided, with the 'me too' movement, the feminist groups, the women liberation groups, the incarceration of men for crimes and drug addiction. Also, the courts since 1969 established a "No-Fault" Divorce Law, giving a woman a legal right to divorce her husband virtually for any reason. Many laws of our land are biased against men, they obviously side with women. Women are gaining so much control over men until it scares men away.

Women in the Christian church are gaining so much unbiblical control until they are being ordained into the ministry with masculine titles. My new book, soon to be published, is called *"The Title Driven Church"- Just Call Me Fred!* I am writing my next book out of my disgust and frustration of what is happening in ministry today among these title seekers, which happens to be men as well.

In addition, the thing that helps to solidify women's rebellion is the fact that most male preachers are afraid and too weak to speak out against it. Instead of being *over* God's local house on earth, they are becoming just a weak mouse in God's church house. Another contributing factor to the man shortage phenomenon - the current divorce and separation rate is so high, coupled with all the above.

Consequently, many men of our day do not have a desire to get married. There exists the MGTOW movement, *men going their own way*. They are so disgusted with the Me Too movement and feminist agendas until they are refusing to get married. Therefore, there is a man shortage in our 21st Century society. There is a man shortage, but it is because of many different negative reasons other than there being much more women in our world than men. Statistically that is not true.

Jesus Spoke About Family Division: *For from henceforth there shall be five in one house divided, three against two, and two against three. The father shall be divided against the son, and the son against the father; the mother against the daughter, and the* *daughter against the mother; the mother in law against her daughter in law, and the daughter in law against her mother in law. (Luke 12:52-53*

In the last days, a woman shall compass a man - this is another scripture that has created a major problem for many Christian men and women in our day. However, it is because of an inaccurate interpretation. *(Jeremiah 31:22)*

How long wilt thou go about, O thou backsliding daughter? For the Lord hath created a new thing in the earth, a woman shall compass a man.

There has been many church ministers and lay people, male and female, who have interpreted this scripture to mean that in the last days which are now, God is doing a new thing, he has ordained the woman to surpass the man. They say this is the reason why the women in our day in the world and in the church seem to be getting ahead of the man and gaining control over men.

First, God never ordained rebellion against his divine orders, which is written in the infallible inspired word. Second, God does not contradict himself, he says what he means and he means what he says. Let's examine this prophetic text and allow the scripture to interpret scripture.

The word there in the latter clause of Jeremiah 31:22 is not surpass, but it is compass. What is a compass? A compass is little gadget used to show you directions of North, South, East and West.

The transliteration of the Hebrew word for COMPASS is mechugah and is a noun (the phonetic spelling is (mekk-oo-gaw') and it means to "CIRCLE AROUND'- to compass. The verb "to compass" occurs frequently in the sense of "to surround" and "to go 'round about."

In short, let me explain what it literally means. The Israelite people, the Jewish people in this text, are characterized as "A Woman". And the Lord Jesus Christ is characterized as "a man'. In Jesus's first coming, His people did not surround him, compass him or embrace him but they as a nation rejected Him as their Messiah.

However, when he returns, it is to judge the world and set up His millennial Kingdom on earth. The new thing on earth is the 1000 year rule and reign of Christ on the throne of David as King over the entire earth. At that time, the woman, God's first wife, the Jewish people, will compass Christ, circle around Christ, embrace Christ as their long-awaited Messiah. (This is a component of the New Thing that will happen during the millennial reign of Christ).

As you study, the pre-text, the text and the post text along with other prophetic scriptures concerning God doing a "New Thing", you will understand better this particular text in its context.

Women should always remember that men, fathers and their spouses need honor and respect. He needs his wife to stand with him and allow him to fulfill his God given role and purpose.

Money Problems and Jealousy Problems: One big problem that many married couples deal with is "The Money Problem". It seems as though there is just not enough money to pay all the bills on time or get those things you need and want, or not enough to have on hand funds for those emergencies, or extra money for those needed vacations. This problem is sometimes connected to the problem of not having a budget or not knowing how to write a budget. Alternatively, *overspending* on thing that the family really does not need - the husband or the wife's spending habits are out of control. He or she repeatedly spend too much on themselves or on their children.

Consequently, frustrations set in, the stress levels go up tremendously which causes an outburst of negative verbal attacks against your spouse as though he or she is the blame for this family dilemma. When the blame game kicks in - one of the mates have to hear and deal with what I call "The If Factor". If you had done so-and-so like I told you to do, we would not be in the mess we are in. It is your fault. Not enough money puts a strain on the love relationship, how can there be romance when there is not enough finance? Romance and finance go together.

Jealousy Problems: The scripture says that jealously is as cruel as the graves. In other words, if jealously is not dealt with properly it can send somebody to an early grave. Cain killed his brother Abel because of jealousy (*Read Genesis 4:8).* Jealousy if not properly dealt with, leads to anger and anger leads to arguments and verbal abuse. In addition, an outburst of anger and arguments can lead to physical abuse - even murder.

Not only that, but anger has a psychological and physiological effects on the person who constantly becomes angry. It may cause the blood pressure to rise to dangerous levels. In addition, it may lead him or her to an early demise.

Some Christian marriages are in real trouble because of that demon called jealously. It is disrupting and destroying their love for each other. Jealously leads to distrust; sometimes there is no real tangible reason for the opposite sex to be jealous of their mate. However, because they grew up seeing unfaithfulness between one or both of their parents or relatives, it leads to him or her bringing that baggage of suspicion and distrust into their marital relationship. It is not long after they are married that these negative feelings of suspicion begin to emerge.

You as a spouse can become so consumed with jealously, until you begin to observe your spouse's every move and activity. When your spouse goes out to shop, the jealous partner is watching the clock. When your spouse returns home, you want to know every detail about every contact or person he or she talked to. Sometimes a spouse will secretly go through their mate's wallet, purse, or cell phone searching for evidence of unfaithfulness.

Jealously will lead to false accusations against your spouse and cause heated arguments. A jealous female spouse has the tendency to distrust all other females around her husband.

Allow me to be transparent, I was twenty-one years of age when I married my beautiful, young, born again, Holy Spirit filled bride (who was seventeen years old). While dating her, we were so in love. Her mom allowed us to go out together sometimes but never without a chaperon. The chaperon was her mom's niece who was also a born again Christian and she was at least twenty years older than the both of us.

During the years when we were dating each other, I never detected any jealousy at all. However, about five years after we were married, my wife began to exhibit a jealous behavior towards me. As far as I can remember, it really started after I became a pastor. I started to pastor a church at the age of twenty six.

She became suspicious of every young adult, female sister in the Lord that was not in our family. She would sometimes ease drop over the phone calls that I would receive from sisters who desired counseling. Although the calls and conversations were innocent in nature, she would at times give me the third degree. It was like an interrogation.
I recall a particular incident when we were at our Wednesday night Bible class, I needed a pencil to illustrate a point. I politely asked did anyone have a pencil. One of the sisters at the class responded and handed her pencil to me to use for the illustration. When we returned home after that class, my spouse began to cry almost hysterically while repeating,

"I wanted to give you a pencil". I became so upset and said to her "How was I supposed to know that you wanted to give me your pencil?"

At this point in our marriage, her jealously had caused me to reach a boiling point. I knew that something had to be done soon or our marriage would not survive this jealousy test. Jealousy will kill a marriage; it will bring death to a good marriage and perhaps an early grave for one of the marriage partners simply because of the mental and emotional stress level in trying to prove your innocence.

There was a method that I used a few times in those early years of our marriage, I would simply get quiet and ignore her. This time I simply told her that she was not allowed to attend any more of our Bible classes when I am teaching. I made it clear to her that I would teach her and our little children at home.

In hindsight, I know now that this was not the wisest way to handle that situation, but it worked for me at that juncture in my life. I must admit that I was somewhat jealous of her as well but never on the level that she was experiencing jealousy of me.

I thank God we were both born again, because we both had a desire and commitment to serve God. In addition, we had a commitment to the marriage covenant to make our marriage work. Through much prayer, we finally had a real positive honest talk about our situation. She confessed that she did not want to live like that anymore and that her jealousy was causing her to become physically sick.
She asked for forgiveness and I forgave her, I also asked her for forgiveness for exhibiting the wrong attitude and she forgave me. Moreover, we both placed our jealousy and my anger on the altar before the Lord. As well, everything else that we were consciously and unconsciously doing that was contributing to the trouble in our marriage. Since then we both have observed God

strengthening our marriage month-by-month and year-by-year. Sometimes we have experienced setbacks, but God has always come through with strength.

Reason to Be Jealous: There are times when a spouse can give his mate a reason to be jealous. For instance, being flirtatious with the opposite sex, hiding your conversation from your mate while talking on your phone, watching pornographic movies, talking pornographic talk with your friend in front of your spouse. This is done sometimes under the guise or pretense of being transparent. Other times it is just plain vulgarity.

Usually, when a born-again believer initially gets saved, they reject all pornography in order to remain morally pure in the sight of God and his or her spouse. In addition, they both desire a pure thought life.

However, in this twenty first century, we are being bombarded daily with images of sexual immorality on TV, the internet/social media etcetera. Moreover, sometimes we let down our guard. By not being watchful, careful and prayerful, we have a tendency to stop protecting our sight and our soul. Consequently, we become weak in the Lord. Your soul consists of your mind, will and your emotions - your mind to think, your will to do and your emotions to feel.

You should always, protect these body parts; your eyes, what you allow your eyes to watch; what you look at is a gateway into your soul. You should protect your ear-gate, what you allow your ears to hear or listen to; what you allow yourself to listen to also affects your mind, will and emotions. Even your nose, what you sniff and smell are a gateway to your brain and your soul. Many are addicted today to a scent or an addictive odor. The Bible teaches us to be careful what we touch what we handle with our hands. A touch can also send a signal to our brain and into our soul.

In addition, the scripture warns us about *feet* that run after mischief. *(Read Proverb 6:18)*

These body parts are the gateway into your soul, what you see, listen to, smell and touch constantly will influence your soul and life. Your mind is the center of your thought life and imaginations. Your will, your volition, is your inner ability to act, to do or not do something; your emotion is the center of your feelings. You need to protect your body functions in order to protect your soul.

When Job's marriage was in trouble, he said: he made a covenant with his eyes not to look or think upon another woman. (*I made a covenant with mine eyes; why then should I think upon a maid? Job 31:1*) Job acknowledges here that what you allow yourself to see is what you will think about.

King David allowed his eyes to look at Uriah's wife taking a sunbath on the rooftop and that look lead him to commit gross sins. (2 Samuel 11:2-14)

Moreover, because of the bombardment of sexually explicit language and behavior in our world around us, we stop trying to intentionally live a morally pure life on a daily basis. Consequently, we become slack in maintaining moral purity and the downward spiral begins.

These are the steps downward; first, we *minimize* the fact that this sin can devastate us spiritually. Second, we begin to *tolerate* seeing and hearing immoral things. Third, we begin to *accept* it as normal behavior. Fourth, we *reject* the idea that this type of illicit behavior is immorally wrong. Lastly, we just might end up *participating* in those things we know are morally wrong and unacceptable by the Lord. Those are the downward steps, minimization, toleration, acceptance, rejection of truth, and participation.

It goes without saying, pornography leads to a sexually impure mind. In addition, inner, impure thoughts generate arguments and distrust in the marriage relationship.

It does not matter whether you are the male leader in a church or a layperson, when you as a husband become dominated by morally impure thoughts, you become a very angry person inside. In addition, your anger leads to arguments with your spouse.

Moreover, if you are not careful you "the male spouse" will begin to mistreat your female spouse like a doormat. (A doormat is that rug at the entrance into the house). Your wife is not a doormat, rather she is the sweet, saved wife/spouse in the house.

You need to keep a short account with yourself, with God and with your female spouse. Resolve early, those issues that are causing dissension and disintegration in your relationship.

You born again husbands do not necessarily need to take anger management classes to deal with your anger, but you must deal with your anger utilizing Biblical principles. You must utilize scriptural instructions as a guideline for the sake of gaining back your freedom, victory, joy and peace in your home. You can get your joy and peace back.

Participating by Watching: Jesus said: when a man looks at a woman with the purpose to lust, he has already committed adultery in his heart - in his soul.

But I say unto you, that whosoever looketh on a woman to lust after her hath committed adultery with her already in his heart.
(Matthew 5:28)

The Apostle Paul said: Who knowing the judgment of God, that they which commit such things are worthy of death, not only do the same, but have pleasure in them that do them. (Roman 1:32)

Watching illicit behavior and things that God describes as an abomination, minimizes the impact that immorality had upon you when you were first born again.

~ PART THREE ~
FAMILY RESPONSIBILITIES AND SOLUTIONS

There are Biblical principles available to guide us to viable solutions for every family problem including child rearing.

Principle Defined: *A fundamental truth or proposition that serves as the foundation for a system of belief or behavior or for a chain of reasoning.*

The first and foremost beginning of every solution is Christ Jesus - Christ in you is the hope of Glory.

To whom God would make known what is the riches of the glory of this mystery among the Gentiles; which is Christ in you, the hope of glory:

Whom we preach, warning every man, and teaching every man in all wisdom; that we may present every man perfect in Christ Jesus (Colossians 1:27-28)

A Father Finding His Purpose

A father needs to find out what his God given place and purpose is and remain in it. A man's first place is living in the purpose and will of God as a father for his family

When God called Abraham to become the father of many nations, he told him his purpose and that purpose is the same purpose that is passed on to every father.

18 Seeing that Abraham shall surely become a great and mighty nation, and all the nations of the earth shall be blessed in him?

19 For I know him, that he will command his children and his household after him, and they shall keep the way of the Lord, to do justice and judgment; that the Lord may bring upon Abraham that which he hath spoken of him. (Genesis 18:18-19)

Notice the purpose for Abraham was first and foremost a family purpose. As the father, his *first* purpose was to guide and command his children and his *household* after him in the ways of the Lord.

This guidance and commanding his children in the ways of the Lord is to be done by teaching and training his children without provoking his children to wrath. God does not want us fathers to forget our family purpose: Paul the Apostle recorded in Ephesians 6: 4; *And, ye fathers, provoke not your children to wrath: but bring them up in the nurture and admonition of the Lord.*

Joshua, the successor to Moses and second leader of the children of Israel purposed in his heart to serve of God, but not only himself his entire household.

"And if it seems evil unto you to serve the LORD, choose you this day whom ye will serve; whether the gods which your fathers served that were on the other side of the flood, or the gods of the Amorites, in whose land ye dwell: but as for me and my house, we will serve the LORD." (Joshua 24:15)

Moses taught the fathers how they were supposed to teach their children. He said in Deuteronomy 6:6-7; *And thou shalt teach them diligently unto thy children, and shalt talk of them when thou sittest in thine house, and when thou walkest by the way, and when thou liest down, and when thou risest up.*

Again, our purpose as fathers go beyond just being a *father,* but it extends to us being a good grandfather, a Godly grandparent, teaching also our son's sons so they can grow up and pass on that righteous, Godly teaching.

Moses in Deuteronomy 4:9 told the fathers what God required of them even as a grandparent and a great grandparent. *And these words, which I command thee this day, shall be in thine heart: Only take heed to thyself, and keep thy soul diligently, lest thou forget the things which thine eyes have seen, and lest they depart from thy heart all the days of thy life: but teach them thy sons, and thy sons' sons;*

God's purpose for the man, especially the men of God is a *family purpose*. As a father, he is to *first* teach his children the righteous ways of the Lord and how to do justly among other people in the world. In addition, he is to teach his entire household, his wife and anyone else that lives in his house.

I preached a message in 2018 and the subject was *Stay in Your Place*. Many men are not standing in their rightful place. In order for a man to stay in his place, he must abide in his purpose, and fulfill his purpose as a father, as a parent and as Godly grandparent. Parenting involves discipline and discipleship.

Train up a child in the way he should go: and when he is old, he will not depart from it. (Proverbs 22:6)

We need to look at the definition of the word 'train' in the Biblical, Hebrew language in order to get clear meaning of what it means and entails. Train in the Hebrew is chanak: (khaw-nak'); it is a verb - the definition is to train up, dedicate. Training a child involves dedicating the child to the Lord, which also involves the disciplining of the child. When the writer says when he gets old he will not depart, this is not a promise, but it is a general statement. The child that receives the right type of Godly, righteous and moral training is in the best position when he gets older because he has something within him to withdraw from.

According to Hebrews 12:7-10, that kind of "child-training" is necessary and important. The God who loves us and who is our Heavenly Father does discipline us even when we are old.

However, Proverbs 22:6 is talking about something even more important than discipline, it is talking about vital, spiritual education that brings a child into definite, real, spiritual experience.

The Hebrew word *chanokh*, translated "*train*," is used as a verb in only three other passages in the Bible. Deuteronomy 20:5 uses it as dedicating a new house. After a person built a new house, the law excused him from service in the army. The soldier was to stay home and dedicate his house because he might die in battle and someone else would dedicate it. The law also excused a man from the army who had planted a vineyard that had not yet produced fruit. He was excused from military duty until the fruit of his vineyard was ripe and he could enjoy it.

Based on these uses of *chanokh*, it seems that training a child involves dedicating a child to the Lord and raising that child in such a way that the child will enjoy the house of God and the things of God.

Later Hebrews used this same concept concerning encouraging a child to cultivate a taste for the things of God. Making prayer, family altars, Sunday school, Sabbath school, church and Synagogue services something enjoyable is the task of both parents and the church.

Our parents and grandparents did these things; they never said critical things in our presence against the pastor or church leaders. Instead, they encouraged us to expect God to answer our prayer.

First Kings 8:63 and 2 Chronicles 7:5 use the word *chanokh* for dedicating the temple of the Lord. Part of this dedication included offering fellowship offerings and consecrating the middle part of the courtyard in front of the temple.

Encouraging dedication and consecration is something that needs to be repeated, again and again. Dedicating the temple was done in the presence of the Lord and all the people. In a similar way, keeping a child in a church where both the Lord and others can observe and encourage their consecration has eternal effects.

I might never have become born again and filled with the baptism in the Holy Spirit if it had not been for the scriptural teaching, encouragement, prayers, and patience of older saints.

The dedication in Proverbs 22:6 is to show the way (Hebrew - derek) the child should go. Derek is often used of God's way, or the behavior that pleases God.

Teaching Begins Before Birth: I believe that teaching begins before the cradle and to the grave. Allow me to say it this way; learning begins before the cradle and it last until the grave.

I have taught for years that training begins before the birth of your child. Training should really begin while your child is developing in the womb of the mother. Through prayer, the mom and the dad should dedicate their unborn baby to the Lord.

I believe that the mom and the dad as Christians should softly sing hymns and praise songs unto God over their unborn child on a daily basis, if possible. In addition, I believe that the parent(s) and or grandparents should read softly the scriptures and quote softly positive scriptures of faith during the mom's pregnancy.

You may ask the question; can an unborn baby hear and understand these things before he or she is born? I am not a pediatrician and have not studied anything concerning pre-birth activities of the unborn. Therefore, from a medical standpoint I am clueless.

However, from my study and knowledge of the Holy Scriptures, they reveal that there is something spiritual going on inside that mother's womb in conjunction with the physical development of that infant.

I am convinced from God's Holy Word, that there is something "Spiritual" taking place in your child's soul and spirit during its development before birth. I believe that there is a spiritual hearing - a spiritual listening happening within that unborn baby.

Why do I believe that? Well let's look at few unexplainable examples:

Example Number 1: The scripture seems to suggest that Timothy's mom and grandmother began to teach and train Timothy while he was yet in his mother Eunice's womb. Moreover, they continued to teach Timothy after he was born and during his young and tender years and teenage years. They dedicated him to the Lord and they intentionally spent precious dedicated time in his development and Godly education.

During a time in Timothy's life when he needed encouragement in the ministry, Paul the Apostle said to Timothy in 2 Timothy 1:5 *When I call to remembrance the unfeigned faith that is in thee, which dwelt first in thy grandmother Lois, and thy mother Eunice; and I am persuaded that in thee also.*

15 And that from a child thou hast known the holy scriptures, which are able to make thee wise unto salvation through faith which is in Christ Jesus. (2 Timothy 3:15)

Child in the Greek is **Teknon:** *a child of either sex*

Téknon (a child living in willing dependence) illustrates how we must all be as little children, as we are receptive to Christ speaking His rhema word within to impart faith.

Nevertheless, the expression used by Paul - "from a child" here is *not* **'Teknon',** rather it is: (**ἀπὸ βρέφους / apo brephous**) – It denotes a child at an early age or before birth.

This word "brephous"- does not make it certain at precisely what age Timothy was first instructed in the Scriptures, though it would denote an "early" age. The word – (βρέφος) brephos – denotes, and some believe (including me), that Brephous refers to a child even before it is born while it is developing in its mother's womb.

Notice if you will, (1) the Greek word "Brephous" - means unborn infant in Luke 1:41 and Luke 1:44.
*41 And it came to pass, that, when Elisabeth heard the salutation of Mary, the babe **(Brephous)** leaped in her womb; and Elisabeth was filled with the Holy Ghost:*

*44 For indeed, as soon as the voice of your greeting sounded in my ears, the babe **(Brephous)** leaped in my womb for joy. (Luke 1:44 (NKJV)*

Notice number (2) Luke 2:16 refers to an infant, a babe, suckling.
*16 And they came with haste, and found Mary, and Joseph, and the babe **(Brephous)** lying in a manger.*

Notice Number (3) The Word "Brephous" can also mean young child or young children (*Acts 7:19 KJV*)

19 The same dealt subtilly with our kindred, and evil entreated our fathers, so that they cast out their young children, (the word young children here is Brephous)

Notice Number (4) that "**Brephous**" for babe also has a spiritual meaning in 1 Peter 2:2

2 As newborn babes, (Brephous) desire the sincere milk of the word that ye may grow thereby: (1 Peter 2:2)

The scriptures are clear, Timothy's mom and grandmother began teaching and training him in the Holy Scripture while he was an infant, possibly before his birth. In addition, because they were Hebrews themselves, they continued in the tradition of teaching and training Timothy in the Holy Scriptures.

Again, the father's duty is to teach his child the Scriptures. In the Old Testament Hebrew culture, one of the first responsibilities of the father in parenting his child was to teach and train his child in the Holy Scripture.

*19 And ye shall **teach them your children**, speaking of them when thou sittest in thine house, and when thou walkest by the way, when thou liest down, and when thou risest up.*

20 And thou shalt write them upon the doorposts of thine house, and upon thy gates:

21 That your days may be multiplied, and the days of your children, in the land which the Lord sware unto your fathers to give them, as the days of heaven upon the earth. (Deuteronomy 11:19-21)

The mother of Timothy was a pious Hebrewess and regarded it as one of the duties of her religion to train her son in the careful knowledge of the word of God. The Jewish writings abound with lessons on this subject.

Teaching their children was regarded by the Hebrews as an important duty of religion, and there is a reason to believe that it was commonly, faithfully performed.

And, although Timothy's father was a gentile, Greek and did not follow these Hebrew customs, Timothy's mom Eunice and his grandmother Lois were Hebrew women. They were faithful and dedicated to training timothy in the ways of the Lord.

The principle here is, to begin training your child when he or she is young and of a tender age, even *before* she or he is born.

There is something spiritual going on before birth; Jacob before he was born wanted to be first. Notice what the scripture says: while he was coming out of his mother's womb, he grabbed hold to Esau's heel.

Genesis 25:21-26

21 And Isaac entreated the Lord for his wife, because she was barren: and the Lord was entreated of him, and Rebekah his wife conceived.

22 And the children struggled together within her; and she said, If it be so, why am I thus? And she went to enquire of the Lord.

23 And the Lord said unto her, two nations are in thy womb, and two manner of people shall be separated from thy bowels; and the one people shall be stronger than the other people; and the elder shall serve the younger.

24 And when her days to be delivered were fulfilled, behold, there were twins in her womb.

25 And the first came out red, all over like a hairy garment; and they called his name Esau.

26 And after that came his brother out, and his hand took hold on Esau's heel; and his name was called Jacob: and Isaac was threescore (60) years old when she bare them.

Training Involves Teaching Obedience: The Jewish writings abound with lessons on this subject.
Children, obey your parents in the Lord: for this is right.
*2 Honor thy father and mother; which is the **first commandment with promise;** 3 That it may be well with thee, and thou mayest live long on the earth. (Ephesian 6:1-2).*

Children today need to understand how serious God is concerning them being respectful and obedient to their parents. I have seen in my lifetime, children who have died as teenagers and young adults because of disobedience to parents.

Training involves teaching your children how to dress:
   a. Unisex clothing is not endorsed in the scriptures. Some children take on the gender and personality that their clothing represents.
   b. Your young or teenage daughter should NOT dress in clothes made for a male
   c. Your son(s) should not be dressed in clothes that represent the opposites sex.
   d. Today there is a gender identity confusion and crisis. We as Godly parents should raise our children to make a distinction in every area of his or her life.
   e. A good Biblical principle is in Deuteronomy 22:5-8 - A woman should not wear a man's apparel, neither should a man wear things that pertained to a woman's apparel. Gender distinction should be exhibited in the way one dresses.
   f. The Bible says even adult women should dress in modest apparel. (*1 Timothy 2:9*)

Training Involves Discipline and Discipleship: He that spareth his rod hateth his son: but he that loveth him chasteneth him betimes.

Folly is bound up in the heart of a child, but the rod of discipline will drive it far away. (Proverbs 22:15 NIV)

Do not withhold discipline from a child; if you punish them with the rod, they will not die. (Proverbs 18:22)

A) Discipline is more than just giving a child time out; it is the use of the rod of correction.

B) The rod of correction does not include physical or verbal abuse.

1. In your disciplinary action always avoid abuse.

2. Do not discipline your child out of anger or when you are angry, when you are angry you are usually out of control. Discipline your child out of love.

3. Do not pick on your child and discipline he or she for every little wrong thing he or she does

4. The purpose of discipline is to break that stubborn will not to kill your child's, hopes, dream, aspirations, purpose and potential.

Training involves love and encouragement: *Lo, children [are] an heritage of the LORD: [and] the fruit of the womb [is his] reward. (Psalms 127:3)*

Children's children [are] the crown of old men; and the glory of children [are] their fathers. (Proverbs 17:6)

And all thy children [shall be] taught of the LORD; and great [shall be] the peace of thy children. (Isaiah 54:13)

At the same time came the disciples unto Jesus, saying, Who is the greatest in the kingdom of heaven?

2 And Jesus called a little child unto him, and set him in the midst of them,

3 And said, Verily I say unto you, except ye be converted, and become as little children, ye shall not enter into the kingdom of heaven. (Matthew 18:1-3)

And, ye fathers, provoke not your children to wrath: but bring them up in the nurture and admonition of the Lord. (Ephesian 6:4)

I have no greater joy than to hear that my children walk in truth (3 John 1:4)

Older Mothers Are to Teach Younger Women

*That they may teach the young women to be sober, to love their husbands, **to love their children,** to be discreet, chaste, keepers at home, good, obedient to their own husbands, that the word of God be not blasphemed. (Titus 2:4-5)*

Parents, especially fathers leading the way, should tell their son(s) that they love him and that they are proud of him just for being their son. The fathers and mother should also say those same things to their daughter(s). In addition, let her know that she is beautiful and special to you as well as being special to God.

Never put them down.; a parent should even ask their child or children for forgiveness when they did not get it right or in some way failed them or accused them falsely or abused them when they were growing up.

Many dads from the older generation owe their children an apology, for failing them in so many areas, and should do so as a true Godly, positive role model.

Training Involves Protecting Your Daughter's Virginity

a) The father was the first one as the head of his house who was supposed to protect his daughter's virginity. He was the one who gave his virgin daughter away in marriage.
   Paul the Apostle wrote to the fathers who had adult virgin daughters that desired to be married, but he the father thought that if he gave her permission to get married, he was in some way committing a sin. Paul said to those fathers; But if any man thinks that he behaveth himself uncomely toward his virgin, if she pass the flower of her age, and need so require, let him do what he will, he sinneth not: let them marry. (1 Corinthians 7:36)

b) The father was responsible also for protecting his sons from marrying a pagan or heathen. Abraham chose a wife for Isaac.

Training Involves Passing on The Fatherly Blessing
In the Old Testament Hebrew culture, it was the custom of the father to pass on the blessings to his first son before he passes away from this life. In the case of Jacob, he was divinely elected before the foundation of the world to receive the blessings. (read Romans 9: 13-14)

The patriarchal blessing was passed on by the father laying his hand upon the head of his son and repeating the blessing prayer/oath. The laying of hands was the act of transferring the blessing. The son that received the blessing became the new head of that family to carry on the blessings and the family legacy.

The fathers according to the Jewish Culture, were to transfer the blessing to the first male child. *Genesis 17:19-21*

19 And God said, Sarah thy wife shall bear thee a son indeed; and thou shalt call his name Isaac: and I will establish my covenant with him for an everlasting covenant, and with his seed after him.

20 And as for Ishmael, I have heard thee: Behold, I have blessed him, and will make him fruitful, and will multiply him exceedingly; twelve princes shall he beget, and I will make him a great nation.

21 But my covenant will I establish with Isaac, which Sarah shall bear unto thee at this set time in the next year.

In Genesis 22:14 – 18, God gave the blessing to Abraham and his seed after he took his son Isaac to offer him on Mount Moriah.

14 And Abraham called the name of that place Jehovah Jireh: as it is said to this day, In the mount of the Lord it shall be seen.

15 And the angel of the Lord called unto Abraham out of heaven the second time,

16 And said, By myself have I sworn, saith the Lord, for because thou hast done this thing, and hast not withheld thy son, thine only son:

17 That in blessing I will bless thee, and in multiplying I will multiply thy seed as the stars of the heaven, and as the sand which is upon the sea shore; and thy seed shall possess the gate of his enemies;

18 And in thy seed shall all the nations of the earth be blessed; because thou hast obeyed my voice.

5 And Abraham gave all that he had unto Isaac. (Genesis 25:5)

B. Isaac Blessed His Son Jacob Instead of Esau:

Genesis 27:26-29 records how Isaac blessed Jacob. 26 And his father Isaac said unto him, come near now, and kiss me, my son.

27 And he came near, and kissed him: and he smelled the smell of his raiment, and blessed him, and said, See, the smell of my son is as the smell of a field which the Lord hath blessed:

28 Therefore God give thee of the dew of heaven, and the fatness of the earth, and plenty of corn and wine:

29 Let people serve thee, and nations bow down to thee: be lord over thy brethren, and let thy mother's sons bow down to thee: cursed be every one that curseth thee, and blessed be he that blesseth the

3 "May God Almighty bless you, And make you fruitful and multiply you, That you may be an assembly of peoples; 4 And give you the blessing of Abraham, To you and your descendants with you, That you may inherit the land in which you are a stranger, Which God gave to Abraham." Genesis 28:3-5 NKJV

5 So Isaac sent Jacob away, and he went to Padan Aram, to Laban the son of Bethel the Syrian. The reason why Isaac sent Jacob away was because Esau was very angry with his brother Jacob. He accused him of stealing his blessings and he sought to kill him. Consequently, Jacob's dad Isaac sent him away to his uncle Laban's home for Jacob's protection.

Although Jacob the heel grabber at birth was a trickster, a scammer who pretended to be Esau in order to receive the blessings from his father Isaac, he was predestined by God to be the future patriarchal head of the Jewish family. It is written in Genesis 25:23, the Lord Speaking to Jacobs mother when she was pregnant with her two sons, *And the LORD said unto her, two nations are in thy womb, and two manner of people shall be separated from thy bowels; and the one people shall be stronger than the other people; and the elder shall serve the younger.*

In fact, earlier before Isaac passes on the blessing, his son Esau despised his birthright and sold his portion for a bowl stew prepared by Jacob. (*Read Genesis 25: 29-34, Genesis 27: 1-46, Genesis 28:1-10 and Romans 9: 13-18*).
The *birthright* was the right to be recognized as firstborn which included many other family fringe benefits.

The passing on of the blessing of the father was of up-most importance because it establishes the house of his children. I believe that we dad's in our generation should lay hands on all our children, sons, daughters and grandchildren and pray that God bless them greatly and protect them wherever they go.

For the blessing of the father establisheth the houses of children; but the curse of the mother rooteth out foundations." (Ecclesiastics 3:9)

Generational Blessings Are an Inheritance

2 His seed shall be mighty upon earth: the generation of the upright shall be blessed.

3 Wealth and riches shall be in his house: and his righteousness endureth forever.

4 Unto the upright there ariseth light in the darkness: he is gracious, and full of compassion, and righteous. (Psalm 112:2-4)

> *We must never minimize the God given role of a righteous father.*

Grandparent's Responsibilities: Fathers and mothers will eventually become grandparents. As a grandparent, the God given obligation is to teach the son's sons the way of the Lord and how to do justice to others. Therefore, you can see that these responsibilities outlined in the Holy Scriptures are extended to the grandparents and great grandparents as well as to the parents.

It is sad to say, but today many parents, grandparents and great grandparents are neglecting their God given duties and responsibility to their children. As a result, many of our children are following the things of this fallen, evil world.
We are living in a sad day when the standard of morality is changing before our very eyes. Immoral or unbiblical behavior patterns and norms are being taught in our education system, from grade school, to junior high, to high school, and in our colleges and universities. Little children are being taught that they can be any gender that he or she chooses regardless of their gender at birth.

One of my granddaughters, who was between three and four years old, came home from her pre-school classes one day and said to her mother: "Mom, I don't want to get married when I grow up." Her mother asked her why. She replied by saying: "A little girl at school told me that girls can marry girls when they grow up".

Our granddaughter, as young as she is, knew that something was disturbingly wrong with that concept. The reason she has that keen sense of right and wrong is because her mom and dad are dedicated Christians. Her grandparents and great grandparents are born again Christians. She is being reared in a Christian home, in a God fearing Christian environment where Christian values are being taught regardless of what is being taught in our secular society.

However, the problem today in our twenty-first century society, many of our children are being neglected, even among some

Christian families. Many of them are being left alone to try and educate themselves, train themselves, provide for themselves, learn morality for themselves. Many have to learn for themselves the difference between Holy Scriptures, secularism, heathenism, paganism and un-godly philosophies. This creates a lot of confusion in the minds of young people.

Our daughters and granddaughters, our sons and grandsons, in many cases are left alone to learn by themselves what a true romantic and dating relationship looks like.
Alternatively, through trial and error, pain and hurts, they are trying to learn how to identify the right person who will someday become their spouse for a lifetime.

Teaching your children, training and disciplining you children is biblical when your children are going through his or her childhood stages of development. The Holy Scriptures endorses disciplinary action for non-adult children, however, when our children are grown, the methods of discipline changes.

The problem is this; some parents do not know or realize when to stop butting in and when to curtail their disciplinary actions. You must realize that your grown up children must now invite you into their situations to talk and counsel with them about certain situations, especially when he or she is not living with you in your home. However, If your grown up child moves into your home to live with you, he or she must honor and respect the chain of authority in your home and must respectfully obey the rules of your home.

I am one who believes and teaches family hierarchy, family humility and family harmony.

~ PART FOUR ~

SINGLE ADULT OF ALL AGES

The Command to Marry

Take ye wives and beget sons and daughters; and take wives for your sons, and give your daughters to husbands, that they may bear sons and daughters; that ye may be increased there, and not diminished. (Jeremiah 29:6 KJV)

In the Old Testament Israeli society, the patriarch, the male, the father selected the bride for his son(s) and he selected the husband for his daughter(s). This was the rule and norm of that society.

The Engagement Period is Before the Marriage Ceremony (The Betrothal)

There were seven stages from the ancient Jewish wedding to the actual wedding ceremony: marriages were arranged.

Stage 1: *The selections of a bride by the father for his son*
   a) The selection and marriage arrangement was made by two families; the family of the groom and the family of the intended bride.

Stage 2: *The paying of the dowry price*
   a) Once the young lady and/or her parents accepts the proposal and receives the dowry price, she was now engaged - it was called betrothed to her husband.

   b) Betrothal in the ancient Israelite culture was just as legally binding as the marriage covenant itself, with the exception that the marriage had not been sexually consummated.

   c) The man's bride was sanctified set aside for her betrothed husband only until the actual day of the wedding. After the wedding, only then would they experience sexual intimacy.

Stage 3: *The waiting period*
   a) The waiting period lasted for one year
   b) During that time, the betrothed husband was preparing a place, a house for his bride

Stage 4: *the seven-day waiting period*
a) After the one year waiting period there was an additional a seven-day waiting period before the actual wedding ceremony. This was done in building anticipation for the wedding.

b) **Stage 5:** *The Wedding Ceremony*
a)   A year later after betrothal, the betrothed husband picks up his bride and takes her to his house.
b)   The marriage ceremony will take place as they stand underneath the canopy called the "hupah". He gives her a ring and they both commit themselves to each other by repeating the marriage vows.

Stage 6: *The Wedding Reception*
   a) The wedding party scheduled by the bridegroom enjoyed with his wife and his guest.

Stage 7: *The Consummation*
a) The husband takes his bride to his house and sexually consummates the marriage.

Examples of the ancient Jewish betrothal and marriage are found in Genesis 24:1-66 and Judges 22:25-26, also in Judges 14:1-7. (Jewish teachers have condensed these stages into two major stages).

Preparation for Marriage

A woman/female, a virgin, had to go through strenuous preparation before the actual wedding day. In fact, it was a custom for virgin daughter to have perfume baths, to soak and have their bodies rub in the sweetest smelling fragrance of their day. Their bodies were given the best beauty treatment available.

In order to get a glimpse into the preparation process of the women prior to marriage, notice *Esther 12:2*. Before a young woman's turn came to go in to King Xerxes, she had to complete twelve months of beauty treatments prescribed for the women, six months with oil of myrrh and six with perfumes and cosmetics.

12 Now when every maid's turn was come to go in to king Ahasuerus, after that she had been twelve months, according to the manner of the women, (for so were the days of their purifications accomplished, to wit, six months with oil of myrrh, and six months with sweet odors, and with other things for the purifying of the women) (Esther 2:12)

> *When a woman is praying to be selected by a man for a wife, she must keep herself looking nice and smelling good at all times. She must continue to do this even after she is married.*

Pre-dating steps: When conducting pre-marital seminars for the single, born again women, I give several steps for them to take before establishing a dating/courting relationship. The single saved woman is advised to ask certain questions in un-intimidating ways.

The single woman is advised *not* to ask these different sets of questions during their first meeting. In addition, some of the answers to your questions can be acquired by other means than asking the potential male spouse.

The First Step - INTRODUCTION:

Get to know the person by name by being introduced to each other, perhaps by exchanging phone numbers. If it seems as though you both want to take this relationship further for example, going out to dinner together or maybe later a dating relationship, then you must move to step two.

The Second Step – INTERVIEW

Get to know the person's true first and last name, where he lives, his relatives, is he born again, how long has he been saved. What is the name of the church he attends, how long has he been a member of that church, where is it located, is he involved in some type of ministry in his home church, the name of the pastor, etc.

The Third Step – INVESTIGATION

This can be done by personal research in order to gather more information about him. This step is the background check; this must be done. The background check can be done on the internet or among his friends or relatives. Where does he truly live, does he have a steady job, how long has he worked for a particular company, does he have a license, a car, a criminal record? Does he live at home, or with a relative, rent or own his own home?

Questions should be asked in a non-intimidating, subliminal way. Does he believe in drinking, going out to secular parties, endorse the LGBTQ community? Does he have any medical, mental or anger or unforgiveness issues concerning being mistreated by someone in his past or the present?

I know you are probably saying; "Wow, I don't want to lock him up, but, if he is the right one for you, you do want to put him on 'lock down' - that is if he truly likes you and the feelings are mutual. If you do not, another woman or sister will eventually put him on lock down.

There is a lot of Internet dating happening in our modern day society. If that is your way of meeting your man, you must be careful and cautious. Many times, the Internet person who is seeking a relationship is a scam artist who is searching for a weak, desperate woman that may have some money in her savings account. As I am writing this book, forty women who met a man on the internet this past year, was murdered by that same man.

The scam artist will flirt and sweet-talk the women until he gets her money. Moreover, most of the time he is scamming more than one woman at a time.

Therefore, this is a note of caution to all you born again, single females out there; follow those three steps before you establish a dating relationship with a man. Moreover, you should look for a real man who is a born again *man of God*, not a woman dressed up in men's apparel disguising herself as a man. Not someone who is confused about his gender. However, first you must know who you are from God's perspective and what He has chosen you to become. He did not choose you to be a thing like a slave. God has elevated womanhood to a place of honor and respect.

The Woman Is Not a Thing

The Old Testament Jewish society was a male dominated society, everything that a man owned was referred to as a thing. All his *things* signified his possessions. Even his wife, his female spouse was a part of his possession and that is why even she was referred to in the Old Testaments as "a thing".

22 Whoso findeth a wife findeth a good thing, and obtaineth favour of the Lord. (Proverbs 18:22 KJV)

We are living under the New Testament dispensation of grace, and a female spouse should never be referred to as a "thing". Under grace, the woman has been set free from that designation or that class position of a husband owned possession. God commanded us not to Lord over his heritage *(1 Peter 5:3-5)*.

When I first got married as a young man with my wife, I interpreted Proverbs 18:22 to mean that she is a good thing because the thing is good. However, through much study I found out that my interpretation was inaccurate.

What is so sad in our day is this; young, saved, church going women are still referring to themselves as "thing". They say: "The Bible says that I am a good thing baby!"

Let us settle this once and for all women, you are not a 'thing'! You are a beautiful, God blessed human being with potential and purpose. Remember, God has elevated you in this dispensation of grace above that designation ascribed to you in the patriarchal society and by pagan religions. Always be careful how you describe yourself, or how you allow or accept how others negatively describe you, because consequently you will begin to act out that description, that characterization.

Now let's get back to singles getting married. To the young, female singles between 18-30, there is a new study out about the brain. The study reveals that the brain is not fully developed until a person is twenty-five years old. Perhaps some of you before that age only think that you know whom you want. Let me give you some good advice, and this goes for the single females of all ages.

1) **Avoid Marrying a Eunuch -** Why? Because a Eunuch does not have any sexual desire for a sexual relationship. Kings in the Old Testament times had Eunuchs overseeing and guarding their Harem. The king knew that he could trust Eunuchs around his women because they had no sexual desires at all.

Examples: *Esther 2:3*
And let the king appoint officers in all the provinces of his kingdom, that they may gather together all the fair young virgins unto Shushan the palace, to the house of the women, unto the custody of Hege the king's chamberlain (Eunuch), keeper of the women; and let their things for purification be given them.

Now when it was Esther's turn, the daughter of Abigail, the niece of Mordecai, who had taken her for his daughter, to go in unto the King, she required nothing. But when Hagai, the King's chamberlain, the keeper of the women, appointed her, Esther obtained favor in the sight of all them that looked upon her *(Esther 2:15)*. This scripture makes it clear that the king's chamberlain was a Eunuch and Esther among all the other women found favor in Hagai's sight.

Jesus Describes Three Types of Eunuchs: Jesus said:

*For there are **some eunuchs**, which were so born from their mother's womb: and there are **some eunuchs,** which were made eunuchs of men: and **there be eunuchs,** which have made themselves eunuchs for the kingdom of heaven's sake. He that is able to receive it let him receive it. (Matthew 19:12 KJV)*

To all you single, saved women, do not waste your time getting involve in a dating relationship with a eunuch-time is too valuable. Regardless of how handsome he is, how well he dresses or how successful he seems to be in the business world, do not waste your time! Move on in prayer and seeking the Lord for a husband that is not a Eunuch. Paul said it is better marry than to burn. If you make the mistake and marry a Eunuch, you will be married and still on fire with no one to cool the flames or put out your fire. You need a husband, a mate, a spouse who is a *"Fire Extinguisher"*.

Alternatively, one who is willing to love and learn how to extinguish your fire. It is also important for women to understand that when a man grow older, most men sex drive diminishes therefore you should not base your married life on sexual gratification but on love and commitment. Remember marriage is a covenant before God.

2) Avoid Marrying a Man Who Has No Direction

How can he help you achieved the fulfillment of God's promised destiny for your life if he does not know where he is going? Women you need a man who does not only have a *prayer* but a *plan*. Even if that plan is in the beginning stage, at least he has some direction in terms of where he desires to go in life.

3) Marry a Kind, Courteous and Respectful, Saved Man

This type of man knows how to treat a woman and possibly his future wife. If he is respectful, he will desire to meet your family and your parents, to get consent concerning dating you.
If he only desires to meet with you secretly then perhaps he is not the right person. Even if you are an adult female, it is wise to consult with your parents. Alternatively, consult an older stable married couple for counseling.

Here is a note to all you parents, after your daughter is full-grown and living on her own, she does not necessarily have to consult with you to get your advice or permission to marry. In the final analysis, it is left up to your daughter to decide. A daughter who loves God and desires to marry a God-fearing man, will respect her parents, grandparents or guardian enough to introduce her potential date and possibly mate to them before establishing any type of romantic relationship. This will help her to avoid many potential problems that she may encounter later if she gets involved in a relationship.

4) He Must Be a Gentleman. He Must Do Gentlemanly Things

Such as:
- Pick you up from your parents or guardian's home
- Escort you to the car
- Slowly opens the car door
- Patiently wait until you are fully in the car before closing the door
- Give you time to put on your seatbelt

- Drive you to a nice restaurant if he is taking you out to dinner

Once you both arrive at the restaurant, his courtesy continues:
- He opens the car door
- Escorts you to the entrance and opens the door
- Wait until you enter
- Escort you to your seat
- Help you with your coat if you are wearing one
- Pull the chair out for you to be seated

Showing courtesy is simply being kind and exemplifying good manners. How he treats you before you marry him is an indication of how he will treat you after you both are married to each other.

5) **Do not be naïve** - Once you have fallen in love, he will continue to be kind, plus, he will send you flowers sometimes or an "I Love You" card or "I Love You" letters. He will let you know often that you are someone special and the woman of his dreams.

6) **Maintain Your Virginity** - Under no circumstances should you consider spending a night or nights together before you are legally married. Since you receive Jesus Christ you are a new virgin in Christ, old things are passed away behold all things has become new. (*Read: Act 15:2, 2 Corinthians 5:17 and Ephesian 5:3*)

7) **Marriage commitment starts with engagement**
In the Old Testament Jewish culture, once a man was dating and became formerly engaged, he was not allowed to be a part of the military, he had to go home and dedicate his house - get his house ready for his new bride.

*7 And what man is there that hath **betrothed a wife**, and hath not taken her? let him go and return unto his house, lest he die in the battle, and another man take her. (Deuteronomy 20:7)*

~ PART FIVE ~
NEWLY WEDS - ONE YEAR HONEYMOON

When the engagement period has ended and the couple is now married, there is a Biblical principle for newlyweds to have a one year "honey moon'. This principal It is found in *Deuteronomy 24:5 When a man hath taken a new wife, he shall not go out to war, neither shall he be charged with any business: but he shall be free at home one year and shall "cheer up" his wife which he hath taken.*

To "cheer up" - the Hebrew verb is "Samach". It encompasses doing things for her that will make her happy, to be gladden, to rejoice, to be joyful, to shout cheerfully.

Saw-makh'; a primitive root; probably to brighten up, i.e. (figuratively) be (causatively, make) blithe or gleesome—cheer up, be (make) glad, (have, make joy-ful), be (make) merry, (cause to, make to) rejoice

Notice, the principle here is - the husband, the male spouse is supposed to be the one in the marriage relationship who takes the initiative, he does things to make his wife happy.

A wife is reciprocal by nature, what you do for her she will in return do these same things back for you. If you do things to cheer her up, make her happy, to make her glad, to cause her to laugh, to cause her to rejoice, to repeat her joy, she will begin to do things for you to cheer you up, to cause you to be happy and to cause you to laugh.

> *Laughter is an action of a merry heart and a merry heart is like medicine - it heals.*

A merry heart doeth good like a medicine: but a broken spirit drieth the bones. (Proverbs 17:22)

A newlywed husband in Old Testament times spent a one year, 'honeymoon' at home with his young wife, cheering her up regularly, letting her know that he only loves her. Spoiling her with the nice, kind, and loving things that he did for her.

Spoil your wife with kind treatment.

With this type of loving behavior and actions, there is no time for the devil and the enemy to get in and spoil your marriage. The first year, the honeymoon year is the 'foundation year'. You must build a great love foundation in order to have a great married life and a great home. A house is only a home when true love is being demonstrated.

Notice that during this first year of marriage, which is the foundation year, the husband is actually meeting some of his new wife's basic and mega needs.

(1) *A Wife Needs Attention* - He meets that need by focusing in on his new wife and constantly doing things for her to make her happy. She needs to know that she is physically and sexually attractive to you.

(2) *A Wife Needs Security* - He meets that need by being home most of the time with her, which makes her feel secure.

(3) *A Wife Needs Appreciation* – He meets that need when he compliments her often.

(4) *A Wife Needs True Love* - She needs you to exhibit *Agape* love which is the unconditional, sacrificial love of God. However, she also needs "Eros" love that is romantic love, romantic desire. She needs to know that you love her and that you only desire her romantically above all others. She needs friendship love "Philia". Your wife needs you to let her know that she is your best friend. In addition, she needs family love (Storge in the Greek).

(5) *She needs confirmation.* Your wife needs you to demonstrate that she, as your new wife and first member of your new family, has first place above your biological family (the husband has this same need).

(6) *The wife needs to cleave to her husband.* To cleave means to cling, follow closely after, to abide fast together. The husband meets this need by leaving his father and mother and cleaving to his wife, making her first in his life. In addition, in ancient Jewish culture, the wife left her family and cleaved to her husband, which was her new family. This principal should be followed in our day if possible, because it will help us avoid negative, judgmental members in each family.

Genesis 2:24 - Therefore, shall a man leave his father and his mother, and shall cleave unto his wife: and they shall be one flesh.

(7) *A Wife also needs Sexual Satisfaction.*

Sometimes the born again wife or born again husband can become so spiritually and heavenly minded until they neglect their spouse's sexual needs. This neglect can cause the neglected spouse to eventually feel unwanted or unattractive. Sexual intimacy neglect is a seed for unfaithfulness. No wonder Paul the Apostle said in 1 Corinthians 7: 5 (KJV):

Defraud ye not one the other, except it be with consent for time, that ye may give yourselves to fasting and prayer; and come together again, that Satan tempt you not for your incontinency. (your lack of self-control)

However, while her husband is doing these things mentioned in Deuteronomy 24:5, he is meeting her needs and she is in return meeting his needs and therefore laying a solid marital foundation to build upon. So many marriages fall apart, because they do not build their foundation well.

I counseled with a couple several years ago whose marriage was falling apart. After about eight years of marriage, they were ready to end the relationship. When I met with them, I sat down and shared a few scriptures with them concerning the *Honeymoon Year*. The honeymoon year gives principles for building a strong marriage foundation.

The wife complained, "We never had a honeymoon year because after we were married my husband went away to school". I told her that all is not lost, start now! Start this week, start from where you are. I counseled her husband and told him that as the head of his wife and family, he is to take the initiative!

I am presenting to you this same solution. To all the married couples that never experienced a honeymoon year...start now!

To you husbands, whatever good and righteous thing that makes your bride, your wife, your female spouse happy, do it! It is important to surprise her with a bouquet of flowers, occasionally send her an "I love you card or letter, give her an unexpected love gift, occasionally take her out on a special dinner date, meet her for lunch, take her shopping, hold her tight, spank her with a soft love spank. Take a 'selfie' with her. Purchase her favorite perfume and give it to her as gift. Do like Solomon did for his wife, sing *romantic* love songs to her, talk sweet love talk in her ears, write a love poem for her only, take some romantic walks and strolls in the park, go on a romantic vacation. Be creative.

There is more recorded in *Proverbs 5:18-20* for young married couples:
*Let thy fountain be blessed: and **rejoice** with the wife of thy youth.*
*Let her be as the loving hind and pleasant roe; let her breasts satisfy thee **at all times**; and be thou **ravished** always with her love.*

Allow me to try to unpack these two verses.

When you see "re" in front of a word it suggests you repeat what you did before and do it again. Other words, what you did before that caused her to be happy, glad, cheerful, and joyful, and be merry and to laugh–repeat it!

The Hebrew word here for rejoice is also the verb "Samach", the root meaning to brighten up, to cause, to make one glad, joyful, cheerful, full, to make one rejoice.

These verses direct the young male spouse to rejoice *with* the wife of his youth, meaning, *do it together!* Youth here is self-explanatory. This does not refer to a *middle-aged* woman or *senior citizen* wife. This is a young wife, a young couple. Young couples can have a lot fun together when you are both newly wedded young people of God.

Let her be as the loving hind and pleasant roe. In other words, Cause her to skip and live above the mundane troubles, like the female deer lives in the mountains towering over problem skipping.

I reiterate, this scripture is for you young married couple. A senior citizen couple may catch a cramp. You young couples should not have to worry about catching leg cramps and body cramps!

This scripture continues to direct the young male spouse on how he can receive another type of satisfaction from his wife. It says; let your young (NOAR) wife's breast satisfy (Chortazo) you at all times. Your young wife needs to understand that God did not bless her with breasts just for nursing babies. Again, the scripture says let only her breast (or Chortazo = fill satisfy) fill you up.

A little, caution to the young male spouse, in your excitement, do not forget that your wife is a human being, handle your new wife softly and gently with care. Be *ravished* at all times with *her* love.

There are two Hebrew words that I want to mention for the word ravished #1: "Labab'-LaVav) and it means to be excited until it makes your heart beat faster.

By implication, the Hebrew word *Labab* means to unheart, i.e. (in good sense) transport with love. In other words, the principal here is for you to love her so much until the excitement of your love causes your heart to beat faster. Especially when you are in her presence or even when you think about her.

Notice: Solomon is *not* writing to you people over sixty. If you folks sixty and over start to feel lightheaded and having heart palpitations when you get around someone that you love, you better go to *urgent care* immediately and get a checked up before you check out. Your fast heartbeat may be a signal of an imminent heart attack.

Also notice, when Solomon used the word ravished here. When he says - and be thou ravished always with her love, he did not use the Hebrew word "Labab", but instead he used the word "Shagah'. And one of the definitions for shagah carries with it the idea of 'intoxication'- to reel, to be enraptured.

Literally, it means to be so in love with your wife, until your love for her intoxicates you. It *enraptures* you to the point, that it causes you to reel, to spin, reel and rock, stagger and wobble like a drunken man sometimes. She intoxicates you with her love. After the honeymoon is over, the spouse is to take the initiative and *repeat* the things he did before that made her happy.

A Personal Testimony of Our Early Marital Years

When I first got married my spouse and I did not experience a honeymoon year, in fact, we had never heard about a honeymoon year. Living in this Western culture, we always believed that once you got married you take a trip somewhere together as a couple for few days or a week. A mini vacation together for the first time after marriage was your "honeymoon". It was during that time as newlyweds you really got to know each other intimately.

We did not take a honeymoon trip until about a year after marriage. All I knew was, I was very much in love with my wife and I wanted to spend the rest of my life with her. I really believe our feelings were mutual.

Although my wife was young, she was a great cook and was always learning and practicing new recipes. I was working construction in those early years of our marriage and she always had a great, full course dinner prepared for us when I returned home from work. We always had dinner together before we had children. Moreover, after our children were born, we continued the practice of having dinner together with our family.

Although she prepared dinner every day, we allocated one evening of the week as our *date night*. Every Thursday evening was our dinner date night. We would not allow anything other than an emergency to keep us from our dinner date. We continued this practice after the children were born.

We loved going out for dinner every Thursday evening. Dating your spouse after you first get married is very romantic and helps in building a solid marital foundation.

During those first few early years as a couple, we often experienced wonderful romantic feelings for each other. We were always together; we did not want to be away from other. In fact, my wife would go to sleep in my arms; we would go to sleep hugged up with each other all night. We never complained about the other snoring too loudly. In fact, just the other night as we were retiring in our king sized bed, she reminded me how she used to go to sleep in my arms on a regular size mattress.

Our first bed had a regular size mattress and that was enough. In fact, in those early months and years of our marriage a regular sized mattress was too large.

I used to tease her and say, "We only need a crib". Those were some great romantic days. We did not have a lot materially, but we had each other and that was all that mattered to the both of us.

Although we did not go away immediately on a honeymoon directly after we were married, living together with each was like a honeymoon. During those early days, months and up to four to five years, we were able to overlook our differences as individuals.

However, once these honeymoon-like years slowly and finally ended, we began to notice some things about each other that we did not fully agree with. We began to notice our differences. Consequently, I began to magnify her negative traits.

What I began to notice was that my wife loved to shop and was constantly looking in a catalog at new clothes and things. She also enjoyed going to the different malls often.

And, although she never pressured me to go buy different things for her, I still felt pressured because I did not have extra money to spend on her for things she liked.

I not only felt pressured, it begins to irritate me when she would scan through the pages of a catalog or go out to a mall. Because later, I would find a list of things written down that she wanted with the cost of each item, which was beyond my small budget.

My irritations escalated into feeling of disgust and periodic anger. Then my anger escalated into periodic fussing at her asking her why she was always looking at things in the catalogs when she knew that I could not afford to buy them for her. The fussing eventually escalated into nit picking. I began finding fault in little things that I disapproved of. I solaced myself by telling myself, well my dad was a "fusser", I take after my dad. Dad used to say; "fussing is my hobby".

Fussing in our marriage was becoming my new habit. My wife would never argue back she would just go into the room and cry. Then I would apologize and make up but, it was not long after I apologized and made up, I was back to the "fussing routine".

After we were married five to six years, as I stated earlier, my wife became very jealous of me and other women being around me. In addition, her jealousy gave me another excuse to be angry and to start an argument.

To make a long story short, when we finally came together and had a true conversation about resolving our problems, she agreed that she was very jealous of me and could not live like that any longer. I agreed that I get angry too quickly with her over small things. We both repented and asked each other for forgiveness.

We marked the calendar and decided that we were starting over again from that date. In hindsight, it sounds kind of funny, each day when I made it twenty-four hours without fussing, I would mark my calendar and basically give myself an A+ and pat myself on the back. Nevertheless, it was working, it was hard trying to change my fussing habit and replace it with only kind words twenty-four hours a day, seven days a week, but it worked. I replaced fussing by not using unkind words when speaking to her but by using only kind words of appreciation.

Although this method worked for me, I suggest to you that there are principles in God's word that are much better than using the calendar technique. One of those principles is; *you can resolve your anger and control your attitude by being quick to forgive.*

*For your anger, keep short accounts with   your wife, others, yourself and God. Repent **ask for forgiveness** each day before the sun sets!*
26 Be ye angry, and sin not: let not the sun go down upon your wrath: (Ephesians 4:26)

1. Be quick to sincerely forgive each other:
And be ye kind one to another, tenderhearted, forgiving one another, even as God for Christ's sake hath forgiven you. (Ephesians 4:32)

2. Be quick to humble one self. Mutual humility, mutual submission is the key to cooperation in a marriage. *Submitting yourselves one to another in the fear of God. (Ephesians 5:21)*

3. A husband loving his wife unconditionally and sacrificially is the key to maintaining a loving, kind and forgiving relationship. In addition, it is the key to resurrecting, restoring and renewing the marriage relationship.

Ephesians 5:21-33 deals with submitting and living the love life unconditionally and sacrificially. The word for love in this chapter is *Agape*, it is the unconditional, sacrificial love of God. It is the *God* kind of love. That supernatural love is given to all us when we are born again in Jesus Christ. This kind of love is infinitely above Eros- (romantic love), Storge (family love) and Philia (friendship love).

When a husband loves his wife like Christ loves the church, he is willing to die for her.

Loving Unconditionally and Sacrificially

25 Husbands, love your wives, even as Christ also loved the church, and gave himself for it;

26 That he might sanctify and cleanse it with the washing of water by the word,

27 That he might present it to himself a glorious church, not having spot, or wrinkle, or any such thing; but that it should be holy and without blemish.

28 So ought men to love their wives as their own bodies. He that loveth his wife loveth himself.

29 For no man ever yet hated his own flesh; but nourisheth and cherisheth it, even as the Lord the church:

30 For we are members of his body, of his flesh, and of his bones.

31 For this cause shall a man leave his father and mother, and shall be joined unto his wife, and they two shall be one flesh.

32 This is a great mystery: but I speak concerning Christ and the church.

33 Nevertheless let every one of you in particular so love his wife even as himself; and the wife see that she reverence her husband.

Notice how the husband is to love his wife. It is in two ways:
1) As Christ loved the church
2) Love her like he loves himself and his own body!

There are some couples that I know personally, who say that they love each other but for some reason they refuse to live in the same house with each other. The scripture teaches that the male spouse is the one who should take the initiative and the necessary steps to make living together the goal of the marriage.

The Bible Give Us Keys for Dwelling Together: when some folks get married, they love each other but it is difficult to live together because one of them is set in his or her own way. The marriage relationship is supposed to grow, that is why it is necessary to lay a solid marriage foundation.

Knowledge in any endeavor is to be gained by study. The husband is commanded to study his wife. Dwelling according to knowledge means that you must study her ways, her likes and dislikes – read her like you read a book. Caution: you will never graduate!

Notice what Peter the Apostle says in *1 Peter 3:7*:
7 Likewise, ye husbands, dwell with them according to knowledge, giving honour unto the wife, as unto the weaker vessel, and as being heirs together of the grace of life; that your prayers be not hindered.

The word for dwell in the Greek below is from vines and from the Strong's concordance: *The Greek word and definition for "Dwell is: μένω ménō, (men'-o) - a primary verb; to stay (in a given place, state, relation or expectancy); abide, continue, dwell, endure, be present, remain, stand, tarry (for) thine own.*

7 Likewise, ye husbands, dwell with them according to knowledge, giving honor unto the wife, as unto the weaker vessel, and as being heirs together of the grace of life; that your prayers be not hindered. (1 Peter 3:7 KJV)

The scripture said to dwell according knowledge. Notice the Greek word for knowledge is *kata gnōsis* (κατά γνῶσις); literally "according to knowledge." The idea is - according to what you know and understand about your wife and her situation. This principal can be ascertained from the context. The word *gnōsis* means both knowledge and understanding, the exact meaning depends on the context.

Thus, the modern version of this verse would mean the man would understand the woman, i.e., what makes her happy, what upsets her, etcetera. That is one of the meanings in the verse, but there are other important meanings that must *not* be overlooked. The problem in this verse is that "knowledge" must be understood in light of the Biblical culture of that day, not our present culture.

The unspoken context of this verse is referring to the biblical culture, the culture in the Apostle Paul's day. In that day, it was very hard on women, especially any woman who did not have the support of a husband or strong family. This is confirmed by the use of the phrase *weaker vessel*.

The woman was considered the weaker vessel, the one who was less capable of sustaining herself without the support of a husband and family. For most of history, women had been abused and ignored by men.

At the time of Christ, for example, a woman's testimony was not even valid in court. That kind of thinking about women ignores the very reason for their creation, that they were to be a helper suitable for man (in contrast to the animals were not suitable helpers to man).

In the New Testament, the teachings of Christ and the Apostles, elevated women in a way that they had never been elevated before. For example, the New Testament formally recognized that a woman had her "own" husband (*1 Cor. 7:2*). This negated the polygamy of many ancient cultures and turned the acceptable sexual dallying of the men in the Greco-Roman culture into sexual immorality.

85

The husband is to live with the wife in a *knowledgeable* way. That means a true knowledge, not the so-called knowledge of women that was accepted as truth in the pagan culture of the first century, that women were inferior to men. The husband, who is a man of God, must ascertain God's perspective and heart for women and also know and act upon that knowledge. I believe that from God's perspective, she is the weaker vessel in terms of her physical body frame and perhaps in other ways because she, *Eve*, fell first to Satan's temptation.

To be truly knowledgeable of his wife, the husband must understand her physically, mentally, emotionally and spiritually. If he does, he will honor her naturally. If he does not, he should honor her because this verse commands him to until his knowledge grows to the point that the honor is an effortless outflow of his knowledge of her.

When you honor and dwell with your wife according to your personal growing knowledge of her, you might never graduate because it seems like you are forever in the school of marriage.

But, when you honor and dwell according to God's perspective, what you know about her and how you place her in an elevated position, one that is also a head of the household, you'll be able to dwell and submit to her sometimes as your spiritual equal.

The Bible says that husbands are to submit to their wives in some areas of the relationship. Paul the Apostle wrote in Ephesian 5:21, *Husbands and wives are to submit to one another.* The scripture also make it clear *and although "men lead the family," the woman is the "house guide', the house despot,* (the household Queen).

Paul the Apostles wrote in 1 Timothy 5:14 *14 I will therefore that the younger women marry, bear children, guide the house, give none occasion to the adversary to speak reproachfully.*

Notice that this scripture refers to the young married woman, the wife, as one who is also ordained by God to *Guide the House.* The Greek word guide via the Strong's Concordance is: *oikodespoteō,* - οἰκοδεσποτέω, which is transliterated as a house despot, (meaning to rule a household). *The husband may be the king of his house, but his wife is the Queen of the house.*

Women of our day are glad to know that God elevated them to a higher status in the New Testament under grace. You are not a doormat, a thing or on the level a non-ruling slave. Along with your husband, God says you also are a ruler of the household, a ruler of your children. You are not a ruler over your husband, but you have equal authority over rearing your children and your household in the fear and admonition of the Lord. Moreover, the scriptures teach that the husband and his wife are heirs together which means equal partners in marriage-joint participant. (1 Peter 3:7)

Again, the scriptures do teach the wives to submit to their own husband, but it also teaches in Ephesian 5:21 that both husband and wife should submit to each other. It says, *submitting yourselves one to another in the fear of God.* Again, the key to family cooperation is mutual submission.

²² *Wives submit yourselves unto your own husbands, as unto the Lord.*

²³ *For the husband is the head of the wife, even as Christ is the head of the church: and he is the saviour of the body.*

²⁴ *Therefore as the church is subject unto Christ, so let the wives be to their own husbands in everything.*

²⁵ *Husbands, love your wives, even as Christ also loved the church, and gave himself for it; (Ephesians 5:22-25)*

Wives, submit yourselves unto your own husbands, as it is fit in the Lord. (Colossians 3:18)

Again, during my family seminars, I teach a three part solution that is necessary for building a great family: One- Hierarchy, Two Humility and Three Harmony.

1) Hierarchy: In every home, there is a chain of authority, children and everyone who lives in that Godly home should submit their obedience to the authorities figures in that home. They should respect honor and obey them and the rules of their house.

2) Humility: I repeat mutual submission is the key to cooperation between husband and wife.

3) Harmony: Harmony is unity. It is working together to accomplished goals in life.

9 Two are better than one; because they have a good reward for their labour. 10 For if they fall, the one will lift up his fellow: but woe to him that is alone when he falleth; for he hath not another to help him up (Ecclesiastes 4:9-10)

Singles Young and Old - Embrace Your Singleness:
   a) This is good counsel for all single adults. A single adult can pray, fast and study the Bible when they desire, without the interference of a spouse
   b) Can set educational and business goals and pursue them without the interference of a spouse or children
   c) Can plan and take vacations without consulting a spouse
   d) Can patiently and prayerfully wait for God to send to him or her a saved, born again spouse. As he or she earnestly seeks God for a mate.

e) Can move forward in fulfilling spiritual goals that you want to obtain in the Lord without the distraction of a dating partner.

f) Can take advantage of the waiting period. Those that wait upon the Lord, he shall renew their strength you shall mount up with wings as an eagle. (*Isaiah 30:31*) Stay calm and pray.

1 Corinthians 7:8-9 (KJV) - I say therefore to the unmarried and widows, it is good for them if they abide even as I. But if they cannot contain, let them marry: for it is better to marry than to burn.

When the Apostle Paul wrote this Letter to the church at Corinth, he was a single man. We know this because he said that he had the right to lead about a mate. Have we not power to lead about a sister, a wife, as well as other apostles, and *as* the brethren of the Lord, and Cephas? (1 Corinthians 9:5)

This was Paul the Apostle's advice to the unmarried and the widows in his day; he said that he would rather that they remain single like him. He said that because of the severe persecution that the church was going through by the Roman government.

However, he continued in verse 9, *But if they cannot contain, let them marry: for it is better to marry than to burn.* The word contain is defined as: hold out, maintain self-control, be content in being single, let them be married, it is better to marry than to burn - KAIO - be consumed with burning sexual desire. *(1 Corinthians 9:5)*

But if they cannot exercise self-control, they should marry. For it is better to marry than to burn with passion. (*1 Corinthians 7:7–9*)

I suppose therefore that this is good for the present distress, I say, that it is good for a man so to be.

Art thou bound unto a wife? seek not to be loosed. Art thou loosed from a wife? Seek not a wife.

But and if thou marry, thou hast not sinned; and if a virgin marries, she hath not sinned. Nevertheless, such shall have trouble in the flesh: but I spare you. (1 Corinthians 7:26-28)

Again, embrace your singleness:

But I would have you without carefulness. He that is unmarried careth for the things that belong to the Lord, how he may please the Lord.

But he that is married careth for the things that are of the world, how he may please his wife.

There is difference also between a wife and a virgin. The unmarried woman careth for the things of the Lord, that she may be holy both in body and in spirit: but she that is married careth for the things of the world, how she may please her husband.

*I am saying this for your own good, not to restrict you, but that you may live in a right way in undivided devotion to the Lord.
1 Corinthians 7:32-35)*

*Don't we have the right to take a believing wife along with us, as do the other apostles and the Lord's brothers and Cephas?
(1 Corinthians 9:5)*

I will therefore that the younger women marry, bear children, guide the house, give none occasion to the adversary to speak reproachfully. (1 Timothy 5:14)

When you read the entire text starting from verse 12 to verse 15, Paul the Apostle addresses how <u>some</u> younger unmarried women who do not follow his instructions to get married, consequently cast of their first faith, become gossipers, busybodies and began to backslide and follow Satan.
Having condemnation because they have cast off their first [a]faith. 13 And besides they learn to be idle, wandering about from house to house, and not only idle but also gossips and busybodies, saying things which they ought not. 14 Therefore I desire that the younger widows marry, bear children, manage the house, give no opportunity to the adversary to speak reproachfully. 15 For some have already turned aside after Satan.
(1 Timothy 5:12-15 NKJV)

Single Young Ladies Finding a Man To Marry - To single women who are waiting for a man to find you and marry you, perhaps the men you know are not looking or searching for someone to marry. Therefore, you should not fill guilty to take steps to find yourself a man who eventually will become your husband. However, seek God first through prayer for guidance and directions.

There is a narrative in the Old Testament concerning the five daughters of Zelophehad; Mahlah, Noah, Hoglah, Milcah and Tirzah. Their father died but had no sons to maintain their father's name or to receive the inheritance. These women went before Moses, the other leaders and the congregation to be granted with the inheritance and get permission to find their own man and get married. The permission was granted. God spoke to Moses *Numbers 27:1-11* concerning their inheritance and *Numbers 26:6* and said *"This is the thing which the Lord doth command concerning the daughters of Zelophehad saying, Let them marry whom they think is best, only to the family of the tribe of their father shall they marry.* As a result, they individually found the man of their dreams and got married according to what God commanded. They were married to a man who was a part of their tribe and not unequally yoked together with an unbeliever. (*Numbers 27:1-11; 36:11*).

Remember what God's word says also in the New Testament about not being unequally yoke together with an unbeliever.

14 Be ye not unequally yoked together with unbelievers: for what fellowship hath righteousness with unrighteousness? and what communion hath light with darkness?

15 And what concord hath Christ with Belial? or what part hath he that believeth with an infidel?

16 And what agreement hath the temple of God with idols? for ye are the temple of the living God; as God hath said, I will dwell in them, and walk in them; and I will be their God, and they shall be my people.

17 Wherefore come out from among them, and be ye separate, saith the Lord, and touch not the unclean thing; and I will receive you. (2 Corinthians 6:14-17)

Caution in Searching for a Man to Marry - Avoid sex traffickers; sex trafficking is rampant in our day. Young teenage girls and women are being kidnapped and being used and abused as sex slaves

Single Men Searching for a Wife - Every single man who is seeking to find a wife, you should search for a virtuous woman. Moreover, to be virtuous should be the goal of every woman single or married because she is the ideal woman.

An Ideal Woman is Strong but not Bossy

In this section, I want to introduce you to the ideal woman. She is called the "virtuous woman" and we are provided a clear look at her, the innermost depths of her character that manifest itself in certain tangible traits (*Prov. 31: 10-31*).

The expression, virtuous woman, is from the Hebrew **ishshah chayil** and literally means *"one of power either in mind or body, or both."* Notice the Hebrews made it clear that this type of woman is not a weakling, a push over, but she is a strong, powerful woman. Her strength can sometimes be misunderstood as being bossy; because she will not allow anyone to make her a "doormat". She not only has a strong mind but a strong constitution. Nevertheless, she is strong spiritually and morally.

Number 1: She is characterized by possessing virtue or moral excellence; righteous; upright

Number 2: She is a woman of women- chaste or virginal-she lives in a state of virginity when she is not married

As one source comments, "She is the perfect housewife, the chaste helpmate of her husband, upright, God-fearing, economical, wise. She is the ideal woman that young wives, older wives, and single women can model their lives after. She is a strong woman but not bossy! Now let's read these several verses about "A Virtuous Woman"

Proverbs 31:10-31

Who can find a virtuous woman? for her price is far above rubies.

The heart of her husband doth safely trust in her, so that he shall have no need of spoil.

12 She will do him good and not evil all the days of her life.

13 She seeketh wool, and flax, and worketh willingly with her hands.

¹⁴ *She is like the merchants' ships; she bringeth her food from afar.*

¹⁵ *She riseth also while it is yet night, and giveth meat to her household, and a portion to her maidens.*

¹⁶ *She considereth a field, and buyeth it: with the fruit of her hands she planteth a vineyard.*

¹⁷ *She girdeth her loins with strength, and strengtheneth her arms.*

¹⁸ *She perceiveth that her merchandise is good: her candle goeth not out by night.*

¹⁹ *She layeth her hands to the spindle, and her hands hold the distaff.*

²⁰ *She stretcheth out her hand to the poor; yea, she reacheth forth her hands to the needy.*

²¹ *She is not afraid of the snow for her household: for all her household are clothed with scarlet.*

²² *She maketh herself coverings of tapestry; her clothing is silk and purple.*

²³ *Her husband is known in the gates, when he sitteth among the elders of the land.*

²⁴ *She maketh fine linen, and selleth it; and delivereth girdles unto the merchant.*

²⁵ *Strength and honour are her clothing; and she shall rejoice in time to come.*

²⁶ *She openeth her mouth with wisdom; and in her tongue is the law of kindness.*

²⁷ *She looketh well to the ways of her household, and eateth not the bread of idleness.*

²⁸ *Her children arise up, and call her blessed; her husband also, and he praiseth her.*

²⁹ *Many daughters have done virtuously, but thou excellest them all.*

³⁰ *Favour is deceitful, and beauty is vain: but a woman that feareth the Lord, she shall be praised.*

³¹ *Give her of the fruit of her hands; and let her own works praise her in the gates.*

Here are ten itemized characteristics or virtues of the virtuous woman in as stated in Proverbs 31.

1. 	**Faith** – A Virtuous Woman serves God with all of her heart, mind, and soul. She seeks His will for her life and follows His ways. *(Proverbs 31: 26, Proverbs 31: 29 – 31, Matthew 22: 37, John 14: 15, Psalm 119: 15)*

2. Marriage – A Virtuous Woman respects her husband, she does him good all the days of her life. She is trustworthy and a help meet. *(Proverbs 31: 11- 12, Proverbs 31: 23, Proverbs 31: 28, 1 Peter 3, Ephesians 5, Genesis2: 18)*

3. Mothering – A Virtuous Woman teaches her children the ways of her Father in heaven. She nurtures her children with the love of Christ, disciplines them with care and wisdom and trains them in the way they should go. *(Proverbs 31: 28, Proverbs 31: 26, Proverbs 22: 6, Deuteronomy 6, Luke 18: 16)*

4. Health – A Virtuous Woman cares for her body; she prepares healthy food for her family. *(Proverbs 31: 14 – 15, Proverbs 31: 17, 1 Corinthians 6: 19, Genesis 1: 29, Daniel 1, Leviticus 11)*

5. Service – A Virtuous Woman serves her husband, her family, her friends and her neighbors with a gentle and loving spirit. She is charitable. *(Proverbs 31: 12, Proverbs 31: 15, Proverbs 31: 20, 1 Corinthians 13: 13)*

6. Finances – A Virtuous Woman spends money wisely. She is careful to purchase quality items which her family needs. *(Proverbs 31: 14, Proverbs 31: 16, Proverbs 31: 18, 1 Timothy 6: 10, Ephesians 5: 23, Deuteronomy 14: 22, Numbers 18: 26)*

7. Industry – A Virtuous Woman works willingly with her hands. She sings praises to God and does not grumble while completing her tasks. *(Proverbs 31: 13, Proverbs 31: 16, Proverbs 31: 24, Proverbs 31: 31, Philippians 2: 14)*

8. Homemaking – A Virtuous Woman is a homemaker. She creates an inviting atmosphere of warmth and love for her family and guests. She uses hospitality to minister to those around her. *(Proverbs 31: 15, Proverbs 31: 20 – 22, Proverbs 31: 27, Titus 2: 5, 1 Peter 4: 9, Hebrews 13:2)*

9. Time – A Virtuous Woman uses her time wisely. She works diligently to complete her daily tasks. She does not spend time dwelling on those things that do not please the Lord. *(Proverbs 31: 13, Proverbs 31: 19, Proverbs 31: 27, Ecclesiastes 3, Proverbs 16: 9, Philippians 4:8)*

10. Beauty – A Virtuous Woman is a woman of worth and beauty, she has the inner beauty that only comes from Christ.

She uses her creativity and sense of style to create beauty in her life and the lives of her loved ones. (*Proverbs 31: 10; Proverbs 31: 21 – 22, Proverbs 31: 24 -25, Isaiah 61: 10, 1 Timothy 2: 9, 1 Peter 3: 1 – 6)*

Counsel for Single Older Women and Older Men

QUESTION: What or who do you want mama? What or who do you want papa?

Sixty years of age in Old Testament, Biblical times were the beginning of the age of wisdom. It was that transition age from the middle age to the beginning of the senior citizen stage.

Older people are supposed to be *much wiser* than you were when you were younger. When you make a decision, you draw from accumulated knowledge and the wisdom that you have gained from various experiences of the past. You are supposed to be sounder and sober minded.

Nevertheless, in our day, many older women and older men over sixty and seventy appear to be young and healthy. Every now and then, a few of them testify how they feel sometimes like they are twenty-one again. Because of these feelings, they desire to date and get married. I want to caution you elderly singles - you can be *"fooled by a feeling"*. When Isaac was an old man and his eyes were dim on the day that he was to bless Esau, he laid his hand upon Jacob and blessed him instead, thinking that he was blessing Esau.

The scripture said when he *felt* Jacob's arm, Jacob felt just like his first son Esau. Therefore, he blessed him with the fatherly blessing. But, he had been fooled by a feeling.

And Jacob went near unto Isaac his father; and he felt him, and said, the voice is Jacob's voice, but the hands are the hands of Esau.

And he discerned him not, because his hands were hairy, as his brother Esau's hands: so he blessed him.

And he said, Art thou my very son Esau? And he said, I am.

And he said, bring it near to me, and I will eat of my son's venison, that my soul may bless thee. And he brought it near to him, and he did eat: and he brought him wine and he drank.

And his father Isaac said unto him, come near now, and kiss me, my son.

And he came near and kissed him: and he smelled the smell of his raiment, and blessed him, and said, See, the smell of my son is as the smell of a field which the Lord hath blessed. (Genesis 27:22-27)

Notice that Isaac was very old when he was fooled by what he felt. Simply because you *felt* like you were twenty-one these last few nights, you are not twenty-one.

A True Story: There was this older saved woman who used to attend the same church that I attended, she was in her eighties, but she was physically strong and very energetic. When she got excited, she would literally run all over the church. She used to show off a little in church by jumping up and down. She would testify how good she felt and how *young* she felt.

It was not very long after a particular day of her feeling young and jubilant like a young person, she became a sanctified, born again *cougar.* She started dating a brother who was in his late forties. They soon got married and approximately two months later, we were having her funeral service. She died and transitioned to Heaven not long after she was married. When she was alive, she often felt like a young woman, but she was *fooled by her feelings.* By being, married to that much younger man was evidently too much activity for her.

When King David was old and on his death bed, his servants got a young virgin for him in order to revive him.

Now king David was old and stricken in years; and they covered him with clothes, but he got no heat.

Wherefore his servants said unto him, let there be sought for my lord the king a young virgin: and let her stand before the king, and let her cherish him, and let her lie in thy bosom, that my lord the king may get heat.

So, they sought for a fair damsel throughout all the coasts of Israel, and found Abishag a Shunammite, and brought her to the king.

And the damsel was very fair, and cherished the king, and ministered to him: but the king knew her not. (His servant knew then that King David was on his way out) Read 1 Kings 1-11

Again, to you single senior citizens, the scripture says to the young married couples to be so in love and so excited over each other until their heart skips a beat and until they reel and rock like they have been intoxicated. If you older singles start to get lightheaded and dizzy over someone, it may be because your blood pressure is dropping too fast, check your blood pressure or call the ambulance, you may need a checkup from the neck up.

Hormonal Imbalance - *another thing elderly people need to consider* - you have passed through those years when your testosterone (sexual hormone) level was high. Now you may need some assistance in order to increase your sex drive.

In the ancient Biblical days, the people of that day used Mandrake. The Mandrake plant was a sex stimulant, an aphrodisiac (*Read Genesis 30:14).* In our day, there are certain foods that are classified as aphrodisiacs. In addition, there is the little blue pill, known as Viagra, as well as other pills. Please mama and please papa, do not take any sexual stimulants until you have visited your doctor and received his medical approval to do so.

You do not want it to be written on your tombstone *"He came and went!"* or *"she came and went in the same hour!"*

Resolving Jealousy, Animosity and Vindictive Attitudes:

Regardless of a married couples age, most couples have to deal with jealousy, animosity and vindictive attitudes towards each other at some point in the marriage. The word of God gives us the answer and solution of how to deal with these sins.

The number one way you resolved this problem is by being kind and forgiving:
*And be ye kind one to another, tenderhearted, **forgiving one another,** even as God for Christ's sake hath forgiven you. (Ephesians 4:32 (KJV)*

Unforgiveness Blocks Blessings: A Personal Testimony

I remember years ago, holding animosity and unforgiveness in my heart. I was living a hurt, mean, vindictive life. I wanted to get even with those who hurt me, mistreated me and lied on me as pastors. The unforgiveness for others was affecting my marriage life and my prayers were being hindered. Because my prayers were being hindered, my blessings were being blocked and delayed. I was hurting so badly inside until sometimes I would preach and use harsh language against the congregation.

I remember one Sunday morning after I had preached, my dad who was also a member of our church, walked up to me and said; "Junior, why are you so mean?"

The hurt and pain inside was almost unbearable, but God begin to deal with me about unforgiveness and letting the anger, hurt, animosity and the vindictive attitudes go completely.

> *You must let it go, because hurting people, hurt people.*

I remember very vividly, it was 1992, I went into my basement, I prayed and told God that I did not want to live with the pain and the unforgiveness any longer. I explained to Christ that I wanted to let go, I wanted to forgive but I just did not have the spiritual strength do so. I began to pray and ask God to help me to forgive all of those who had wrong me. I asked him to please give me the strength to forgive. I told God while praying that I wanted to be free totally of unforgiveness. I said to him Lord, "Please make me the channel of your divine forgiveness". With tears streaming down my face, I begged Jesus to forgive my enemies through me.

As I prayed, I began to feel a release, a freedom on the inside that I had not felt for a long time. I also began to feel victory over unforgiveness in my soul, to the point that I began to say repeatedly, Lord, I forgive them. It is unexplainable what took place that day; it was like I was emptying myself of a weight; it was like I was receiving an inner cleansing and washing of my soul. The bondage was broken at last. I begin to dance and shout all over the place in my basement. It was a "forgiveness revival".

It has been over two decades ago since God delivered me and freed me of unforgiveness. I am so thankful for my deliverance. I got my joy and peace back. In addition, the doors of God's blessings swung wide open and God has been blessing me and our family with conditional and unconditional blessings ever since. Thank God, I am free.

~ PART 6 ~

BUDGETING - Solving the Money Problem

No Finance – No Romance

Whether you are single or married, you need to have a set budget. Without a budget, you will never be able to give as you should give, save or invest as you should invest. Without a budget, you will have the tendency to spend and over spend on unnecessary things.

Without a budget, you will never be able to reach your major goals in life, like investing, owning your own car, owning your own home, completing certain educational and business goals, periodically taking a nice trip or vacation. It can become very expensive to fulfill some of your desires and heartfelt goals.

It costs money to pay the mortgage payment, rent, utility bills, home up-keep, cleaners, groceries, clothing, insurance bills, internet bill (or its equivalent). If you own a car, not only do you need gas and oil, but also you need money for maintenance of your car plus automobile insurance, money for travelling - you get the picture.

For married couples, there are added expenses. Moreover, if the husband desires to maintain his position of leadership as *the male Spouse Over the House,* you must budget in order to pay those bills on time so you can have some extra money on hand and an excellent credit rating.

As the male spouse over the household, in order to do those things that we mentioned in the last chapter about keeping your female spouse happy, you need some finances. "No Finance, No Romance!"

Moreover, if you have children, the living expense escalates. Without a budget, you will always find yourself borrowing from Peter to pay Paul. You will never seem to have enough to make ends meet.

I know some people who do not budget and almost every week, three days after they get paid, they end up broke. It becomes very frustrating to them because things they want to do in life cost money, and it seem like they just cannot get off the ground, they just cannot get ahead.

If you are experiencing that type of situation in your life and you have a job or money coming in, you need a budget. A budget can help you to turn things around; with much planning, a budget can help you become debt free.

Jesus, while on earth, gave us instructions about budgeting.

28 For which of you, intending to build a tower, sitteth not down first, and counteth the cost, whether he have sufficient to finish it?

29 Lest haply, after he hath laid the foundation, and is not able to finish it, all that behold it begin to mock him,

30 Saying, this man began to build, and was not able to finish.

(Luke 14:28-30 KJV)

Therefore, the principle of budgeting is derived from the Holy Scriptures. Jesus asked the question, which one of you would get involved with any major project, and not sit down first and count up or add up the cost, so once you have started the project you will know beforehand whether you will have enough funds available to finish the project?

Again, the principle here; is the principal of counting the cost, adding the cost of everything, itemizing systematically "outlining your budget".

Many mega ministers violate this principle of counting the cost. *They failed to make sure first,* that they have enough funds to start and complete the project. Instead, they start a new project and then solicit or beg for funds from the public to complete the project or to complete various phases of the project. But, Again Jesus said count up the cost, add up the cost first.

If you get paid on a weekly basis, your budget will be based upon a weekly budget outline. If you get paid on a monthly basis, it will be based upon a monthly budget outline. You write out and outline your budget beforehand so you will not be stressing at the end of each week.

In writing out a weekly budget you always insert the date at the head of your outline. You start by itemizing everything systematically: your income, your out-go which includes: your tithe, your offerings, monetary gifts, your bills, your savings, your emergency fund, your investment amount (if there is any).

Write down your income first, your tithe, your gifts, your bills and your savings next in that order. This is what I describe as "outlining a budget".

With a well-written outlined itemized budget, you know what funds you have on hand; you know what is coming in on a weekly and monthly basis. In addition, you know what your weekly and monthly expenditure is, except for those unexpected emergencies. *Avoid overspending!*

Sample Budgets: If you do not know how to outline a budget, try and get someone to show you how to do it. Or allow someone to do it for you. On the other hand, you can go to Google and do a search for the type of budget spreadsheet or worksheet you need. Download that spreadsheet into your computer files. Print it out in order to use it on a regular basis. Or, you can fill it out and saved it to your computer files. These are simple instructions, but I do not take it for granted that every person knows what to do.

If you do not know how to go online and Google the information you need, simply get someone to help you. I visited three sites this morning, you can do the same. Again, go to the Google website and search for: 10 Free Household Budget Spreadsheets for the current year, or a household budget worksheet, or a monthly business budget template. Plan to practice good stewardship over the monetary blessings which God is blessing you with.

Stewardship: In budgeting your money, you are practicing being a good steward over what God is blessing you with. I also budget my time by outlining a daily schedule of what I need to do; prayer time, study time, meditating on God's word and writing books is very important to me.

In addition, I outline a weekly, monthly and annual schedule of things that I desire to do in ministry for the Lord. Without a written budget or a schedule, things that need to be done will be neglected. Paul the Apostle said in *1Corinthians 4:2 Moreover, it is required in stewards, that a man be found faithful.*

Jesus Christ, while he was on planet earth, he taught his disciples about Stewardship by speaking Parables to them: And he said also unto his disciples, there was a certain rich man, which had a steward; and the same was accused unto him that he had wasted his goods.

2 And he called him, and said unto him, how is it that I hear this of thee? give an account of thy stewardship; for thou mayest be no longer steward.

3 Then the steward said within himself, what shall I do? for my lord taketh away from me the stewardship: I cannot dig; to beg I am ashamed.

4 I am resolved what to do, that, when I am put out of the stewardship, they may receive me into their houses.

5 So he called every one of his lord's debtors unto him, and said unto the first, How much owest thou unto my lord?

6 And he said, an hundred measures of oil. And he said unto him, take thy bill, and sit down quickly, and write fifty.

7 Then said he to another, And how much owest thou? And he said, An hundred measures of wheat. And he said unto him, take thy bill, and write fourscore.

8 And the lord commended the unjust steward, because he had done wisely: for the children of this world are in their generation wiser than the children of light.

9 And I say unto you, make to yourselves friends of the mammon of unrighteousness; that, when ye fail, they may receive you into everlasting habitations.

10 He that is faithful in that which is least is faithful also in much: and he that is unjust in the least is unjust also in much.

11 *If therefore ye have not been faithful in the unrighteous mammon, who will commit to your trust the true riches?*

12 *And if ye have not been faithful in that which is another man's, who shall give you that which is your own?*

13 *No servant can serve two masters: for either he will hate the one and love the other; or else he will hold to the one and despise the other. Ye cannot serve God and mammon (money). (Luke 16:1-13)*

Parable of Talents

14 *For the kingdom of heaven is as a man travelling into a far country, who called his own servants, and delivered unto them his goods.*

15 *And unto one he gave five talents, to another two, and to another* **one;** *to every man according to his several ability; and straightway took his journey.*

16 *Then he that had received the five talents went and traded with the same and made them other five talents.*

17 *And likewise he that had received two, he also gained other two.*

18 *But he that had received one went and digged in the earth, and hid his lord's money.*

19 *After a long time the lord of those servants cometh, and reckoneth with them.*

20 *And so he that had received five talents came and brought other five talents, saying, Lord, thou deliveredst unto me five talents: behold, I have gained beside them five talents more.*

21 *His lord said unto him, well done, thou good and faithful servant: thou hast been faithful over a few things, I will make thee ruler over many things: enter thou into the joy of thy lord.*

22 *He also that had received two talents came and said, Lord, thou deliveredst unto me two talents: behold, I have gained two other talents beside them.*

23 *His lord said unto him, well done, good and faithful servant; thou hast been faithful over a few things, I will make thee ruler over many things: enter thou into the joy of thy lord.*

24 *Then he which had received the one talent came and said, Lord, I knew thee that thou art an hard man, reaping where thou hast not sown, and gathering where thou hast not strawed:*

25 *And I was afraid and went and hid thy talent in the earth: lo, there thou hast that is thine.*

26 *His lord answered and said unto him, thou wicked and slothful servant, thou knewest that I reap where I sowed not, and gather where I have not strawed:*

27 *Thou oughtest therefore to have put my money to the exchangers, and then at my coming I should have received mine own with usury.*

28 *Take therefore the talent from him and give it unto him which hath ten talents.*

29 *For unto everyone that hath shall be given, and he shall have abundance: but from him that hath not shall be taken away even that which he hath.*

30 *And cast ye the unprofitable servant into outer darkness: there shall be weeping and gnashing of teeth. (Matthew 25:14-30)*

The principle here is to invest, in order to gain *more* with what God has blessed you with.

Finally, if when you married, you were already established in a great business or had investments and a large savings account, and you married without a pre-nuptial agreement, seek to acquire a post-nuptial. You need to protect those assets that God blessed you with.

Do not become just a male mouse in your house but the male *Spouse Over Your House*, one who is committed to doing God's will, God's way in all things.

BIBLIOGRAPHY

===

Unless otherwise noted, Scripture quotations are taken from the Holy Bible the KJV King James Version, The NIV (New International Version), the TLB (Life Application Bible).

10 Free Household Budget Spreadsheets for 2019.
https://christianpf.com/10-free-household-budget-spreadsheets

Barnes. "Notes on The Bible on Brephous"
https://biblehub.com/commentaries/barnes/2_timothy/3.htm

https://www.studylight.org/commentaries/bnb/psalms-8.html

Biblical Symbols - Symbolism is the Vehicle of Revelation.
biblesymbol.com/what-are-bible-symbols/

Chanak. "Train a Child". *https://biblehub.com/hebrew/2596.htm*

Clarke, Adam. "Commentary on Proverbs 31:4". "The Adam Clarke Commentary".
https://www.studylight.org/commentaries/acc/proverbs-31.html.
(1832).

Definition of Spouse. Dictionary. *Vocabulary.com*

Drachman, Bernard; Jastrow, Marcus. Notes on BETROTHAL:
(BETROTHAL - אירוסין in Talmudic Hebrew). *http://instpaper.com*

Dr. David Elgavish, Department of Bible - Bar-IIN University. *The Story of the Marriage of Isaac and Rebekah* (Gen. 24)

"Free Proverbs 31 Printable Bible Study".
www.revisedenglishversion.com/1-Peter/3/7

Greek Definition of Child (Teknon). Strong's Concordance 5043
http://Biblehub.com – Pg 51.

Horton, Stanley M. "Enrichment Journal" (Pgs. 47-49)

Metaphor Reference. *Wikipedia.com*
Strong's Concordance. "Samach, Chortazo, Noar"

The Proverbs 31 Woman. *https://avirtuouswoman.org/10-virtues-of-the-proverbs-31-woman/*

Contact Information

==

Feel free to contact Dr. Fred Jerkins Jr. at any of the below contact methods:

Personal Website:
www.drfredjerkins.com

Email Contact
drfredjerkinsbooks@gmail.com

Mailing Address:
Fred Jerkins Ministries
PO. Box 595
Pomona, New Jersey 08240

www.ingramcontent.com/pod-product-compliance
Lightning Source LLC
Chambersburg PA
CBHW062003040426
42447CB00010B/1878